friends and fellow students

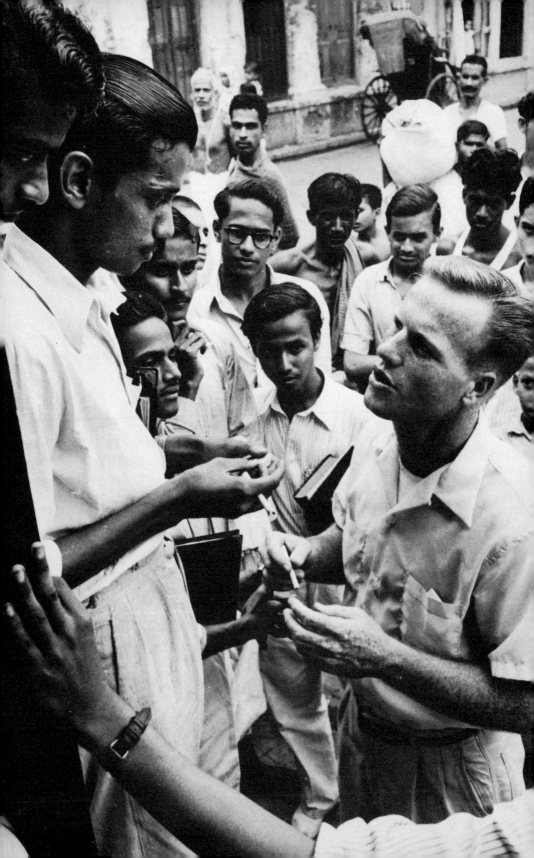

friends and

fellow students

THOMAS BRUCE MORGAN

photographs by BOB LERNER
Look Magazine

THOMAS Y. CROWELL COMPANY, NEW YORK

*This book is for my mother and father
and for Joan*

author's foreword

FROM KIPLING TO CHESTER BOWLES, ENGLISHMEN AND AMERICANS have often taken inspiration from India and have written hundreds of books about her—loving books, angry books, hopeful books. Ten minutes after I landed in Bombay on a magazine assignment, India had her usual effect—I began making notes for a book of my own. But there was a difference. Even though the setting was India, I was traveling with twelve American college students and most of the inspiration came from them. When the magazine story appeared, the most frequent criticism was that "it didn't say enough about India." My only answer was that its purpose was to say something about America. The same is true of this book.

Many people gave me valuable help and advice in the preparation of my manuscript, but I am especially indebted to four people. Three are editors of *Look* Magazine—Gardner Cowles, Daniel D. Mich, and William B. Arthur—who together made it possible for me to go to India in the first place. I am grateful to Cowles Magazines, Inc., for the permission to include here the *Look* photographs taken by my good friend and companion, Bob Lerner.

The fourth person is Joan Morgan, who functioned steadfastly on my behalf as literary critic and wife. None of these people, however, are to be held responsible for the statements of fact and opinion herein. For better or worse, all that follows is my own doing.

T. B. M.

New York, April, 1956

contents

illustrations

Following page 116

Ron Pengilly, Sandy Ragins, Bob Stein, Patti Price, and George Wakiji walk with university students along Chowringhee Road in Calcutta.

At Santoshpur, the Calcutta team works on its dispensary with the help of refugee children and friendly students.

Ron Pengilly plays horse-and-rider with a new young friend.

In World War II battlement, George Wakiji chips brick for the dispensary floor.

Coeds from the University of Calcutta pass bricks to Sandy Ragins.

Mary Ann Buford and Patti Price play Drop the Hankie with refugee children.

Gram Guenther has a proud moment at the dedication of the dispensary.

Mary Ann Buford leads her playmates in London Bridge.

Bob Stein and Patti Price keep "Coffee House hours" in Calcutta.

Sandy Ragins at Howrah Station gets a farewell gift of flowers from university students.

Patti Price argues with a Sikh student on College Street corner.

PART **1** *India, Here We Come!*

1

ABOUT 400,000 INDIAN BOYS AND GIRLS WERE ATTENDING THE COLLEGES AND UNIVERSITIES OF INDIA IN THE SUMMER OF 1955, EACH ONE WITH AN IMAGE OF AMERICA IN HIS mind. Most of these images, friendly or unfriendly toward America, were second-hand. . . .

In that summer, with photographer Bob Lerner, I was assigned by *Look* magazine to a story about twelve students from the University of California at Los Angeles and their two adult leaders on a venture known as Project India. The purpose of the project was to meet with a significant segment of the Indian student community, to reassure the friendly, to befriend the unfriendly, and to leave behind a first-hand impression of what they, as Americans, were really like.

The originator and leader of Project India was Miss Adaline Guenther, a tall, thin, angular lady with white hair and clear blue eyes behind rimless glasses. She was in her late fifties, and everyone who knew her called her "Gram."

We first met that spring in Westwood, California, just off the U.C.L.A. campus, at the new building which housed the University Religious Conference—a privately financed union of all religious groups at the school. I learned that Gram was the daughter of a Methodist minister and a Phi Beta Kappa graduate of Ohio Wesleyan. She went to work for U.R.C. in 1928, the year it was founded. When Dr. Thomas Evans, the founder, died in 1945, Gram became director of U.R.C., with the title of executive secretary, and carried on the various good works of the union—a campus religious emphasis week, a university summer camp for underprivileged children, a year-round program of discussion groups and seminars, and so on.

Gram was bright, brisk, and tense with compressed energy. After looking me over, she sat me down and told me how Project India started. In January, 1952, a Presbyterian minister, Dr. James H. Robinson, a Negro, lectured to an audience of U.C.L.A. students about his recent trip to India. He said Communist propagandists were spreading the usual lies about America, but what alarmed him was how many Indians believed them. It would do

3

no good to complain about it, Robinson said, unless Americans were willing to go to India and personally do something about it. Our only hope was the person-to-person approach.

Later, a few of Robinson's listeners discussed these revelations with Gram Guenther. One inspired student had the idea that they actually might go to India and personally set the record straight, if only they could find the money for their plane fare. They might at least do some good among Indian college students, with whom they would have much in common.

The idea was so preposterous that the money was found. Winthrop Rockefeller put up $15,000 in 1952, then the Ford Foundation put up $23,000, $25,000, and $25,000 for the years 1953, 1954, and 1955, respectively. In the summer of 1952, when our schools were on vacation and Indian schools were in session, the first team went abroad, led by Gram Guenther, and astonished itself by making new friends for America wherever it went. The next summer, Project India was welcomed even by the United States State Department, which had not been enthusiastic when the idea was first announced. At the end of the third summer, Gram could report with pride that the first three Project India teams had met with more than 100,000 Indian college students!

The second adult leader of Project India was a 33-year-old Burbank High School English teacher named Bob Jaffie. He was six feet tall with blazing red hair, freckles, a ski-jump nose, and shell-rimmed glasses. Jaffie had been a friend of Gram's since his own college days at U.C.L.A., where he distinguished himself as president of the student body in 1944.

Jaffie had missed Project India, 1952, but had gone along in 1953 and 1954. While he was abroad, his wife, Margaret, and their three-year-old daughter, Nancy, remained at home in their neat brick bungalow in Burbank. A few nights after my first meeting with Gram, I had dinner there with the Jaffies. Margaret told me that she wrote her husband every day he was away. She numbered each letter so that at the end of the summer they would know which letters were missing. It sometimes took three weeks for a letter to catch up with Jaffie in India, but so far, in two summers, he had received every letter she wrote.

TOGETHER, Gram Guenther and Bob Jaffie had selected the twelve students for Project India, 1955. Gram's call for volunteers late in February brought one hundred applicants to the first meeting at the U.R.C. building. Here, members of the 1954 team retold their Indian adventures, answered questions, and, with Gram and Jaffie, circulated around the room looking for students that seemed to be likely prospects. After three such meetings, Gram notified twenty-four of the applicants that they had survived the first elimination trial. Now they had a fifty-fifty chance. Each one was assigned a special report on "India's economy" or "India's army" or "India's foreign relations"; a total of twenty-four different papers were prepared and presented to the group as a whole during three months of weekly and semi-weekly seminars.

While this was going on and while the applicants were attempting, at the same time, to maintain their regular studies, the U.C.L.A. psychology department prepared a three-hour test for them. It was designed to determine "emotional maturity" as well as "social and psychological adaptability." Finally, each applicant was asked to write down the five people in the group with whom he or she would like to travel for the summer.

It was a very complicated business!

In the end, Gram and Jaffie considered the results of all the tests and observations, added their own subjective feelings, and chose twelve students—eight boys and four girls, including two Negro students, two Nisei students, and eight white students.

Having run the gauntlet, the twelve were shot for yellow fever, cholera, and smallpox. Gram made it clear to them that she was as much concerned with their health as with any other single thing. Because of monsoon rains, heat, and high humidity, past summers had not been easy. Severe cases of dysentery, rashes, fevers, and lost weight were common. One boy, his resistance low at the end of the trip, was stricken with polio in Paris on the way home. No one, not even the boy with polio, was permanently afflicted, yet Gram was supremely cautious. She was asking a lot of twelve innocent undergraduates, though she was asking even more from herself—a *fourth* time, late in life, and with full knowledge of what discomforts lay ahead. The team, therefore, was required to read and digest her long list of health rules, which ranged from the science of water purification to the art of peeling tangerines without contaminating the inner fruit.

Thus prepared, Gram Guenther, Bob Jaffie, and their twelve students flew to India—via Washington, D.C. The plane tickets— as well as hotel bills, food, medicines, and train and bus fares— were paid for with the Ford Foundation's money. To pay personal expenses, each student had a minimum of two hundred dollars of his own money. In addition, Gram and Jaffie carried money which would be converted into rupees and given away by the California students at appropriate times for worthy causes in India. This latter sum of money had been raised by Project India, 1954, in a series of speaking engagements before civic groups in California and in other fund-raising activities on the U.C.L.A. campus. They had been pledged to this type of work for the full school year following their return to America, and the 1955 group was pledged to do the same for Project India, 1956.

They landed in Washington after an overnight TWA tourist flight from the West. Lerner and I met them at the State Department where, on a very hot day, we sweltered through a six-hour briefing session. In the evening it rained, and we were able to enjoy ourselves at the dinner given for Project India at the home of the Indian Cultural Affairs Officer, Professor M. S. Sundaram.

Among the Professor's guests was Douglas Ensminger, director of the Ford Foundation's work in India and a close observer of Gram's previous groups. After dinner, Ensminger spoke briefly:

"It will be easy for you to become irritated, because there are many differences between you and the students of India. But you must find a way to communicate with each other. Be sure you consider India's problems in terms of what you would do to solve similar problems in the United States. Try to understand India's position.

"For example, imagine that Canada was Russia and that Mexico was Red China and that we were India. Then, consider India's foreign policy. . . .

"Think of India in two parts. It is a very old culture. But it is also a very new nation. This will help you understand conditions you see there. You can despair at the privation and filth. Or you can look at the people of India and realize that they are India's richest resource—its greatest hope."

For the California students, Ensminger's talk brought India into focus in the real world. India was no longer a place on the map; it was where they were going. Three days later, they arrived.

From experience, Gram had learned that twelve students in one place make an unwieldy group, so the project was divided into two six-member teams, with colleges to visit in widely separated areas of the Indian sub-continent. Gram and Jaffie had shuffled the names of the twelve students over and over until they arrived at these combinations, which seemed best for the assignments involved.

Gram's team—Sandy Ragins, Patti Price, Ron Pengilly, Mary Ann Buford, George Wakiji, and Bob Stein—would go east to Nagpur, a city in central India, live for a week, and then move on to Calcutta for a stay of five weeks.

Jaffie's team—Ed Peck, Jerry Lewis, Everett Brandon, Ruth Taketaya, Rosemary Wooldridge, and Joe Michels—would go south to Travancore-Cochin state, to such college towns as Trivandrum, Kottayam, and Ernakulam, the latter being the primary seaport on the Malabar Coast.

At mid-summer, the teams would meet again in Calcutta, exchange leaders, take a few days' rest, and go on to college towns in the north.

Ten days after the teams had gone their separate ways, Bob Lerner and I arrived in India. We had five weeks to fulfill our assignment and chose to spend the first two weeks of that time with Jaffie's team. He had wired us his team's schedule, and we planned to meet him in the town of Kottayam. To get there, Lerner and I flew from Bombay to Ernakulam on the Arabian Sea less than two hundred miles from the southern tip of India. Then we boarded a southbound express bus for Kottayam, fifty miles down the Malabar Coast. . . .

THE bus raced down a single lane highway with its window flaps standing straight out like a running dog's ears and the monsoon rain pouring in. Sitting by the window was like being under a shower, while next to me sat Lerner, quite dry, with his camera bag perched on his lap. He was a worried-looking, even-tempered man, and like me, was twenty-eight years old. Both of us could pass for older college students and rarely needed to explain our presence with Project India.

Our bus driver was an angry, bare-footed man. He was angry at the narrowness of the road, at the driving rain, and at the total unconcern of the people walking squarely in the middle of the road—the straight, lithe women with rings in their ears and white cotton saris clinging wetly to their bodies; thin, short men wearing their shirt-tails out and their *dhotis* pulled up and tied above their knees (a *dhoti* is a piece of white cotton cloth, which most Indian males wear, either down to their ankles like a skirt or tied above the knees like bloomers, and which stays up without belt or suspenders); little boys in white loincloths; and little girls in red, green, and blue blouses and long wrap-around skirts.

They were a beautiful sight! But our bus driver swore at them all and honked his klaxon incessantly. When we approached, the adults glided onto the narrow shoulder of the road, but the children waited until the last instant before scampering out of the way.

The bus itself had to take to the shoulder when a car came toward it or when a contented cow would not move out of the way. Indian cows are sacred and have been so well-treated for so long that most of them are quite fearless. Once a slow-moving elephant and its young rider cheerfully blocked the road.

Soaking up the rain on both sides of the highway, there were thick tropical forests of palm trees and exotic evergreens. Red hibiscus and yellow gardenias grew side by side, each adding to the brilliance of the other. The countryside looked like a Gauguin painting, except that the women wore no flowers in their hair.

The forests were interrupted by broad rice fields, and on the low hills beyond the paddies we could see tea trees growing in clipped precision. The monsoon seemed to be refreshing every thing and every one: a man scrubbed his bullock in a pool of yellow water; a young woman carried a brass water jug on her head with the grace of a dancer; a happy-looking man on a bicycle pumped past us heading north, the handle of his umbrella hooked onto the back of his collar and the umbrella dangling unused on his back.

Half way to Kottayam, the bus stopped in a small town. We stretched our legs in the depot and I began chatting with a tall, light-skinned Indian. He wore a collarless shirt with a single gold collar button. Suddenly, a group of beggars, a blind man and two cripples, besieged us. Each was led by a small boy in rags holding out his hand and pleading, "Sahib, Sahib, Sahib! Baksheesh, baksheesh, baksheesh!"

The Indian with the gold collar button took my arm and turned me away from the beggars. He said:

"We do not like to encourage beggars in India. The government takes care of these sick people if they go to the places set aside for them. No one has to beg in India." The man spoke English carefully, but the tone of his voice was that of a man ashamed of a member of his family—the beggars embarrassed *him*. In his voice was pride, defensiveness, self-consciousness, and the sense that all these problems could be solved now. Indeed, he was saying, "We're not children anymore," and he was embarrassed at this evidence to the contrary.

The bus driver sounded his klaxon, and the beggars followed us in the rain to the bus. I tried to look very stern as I climbed aboard, but the small boys had given up by then and were giggling.

Bob Lerner agreed to take the seat by the window for the remainder of the trip if I would hold his camera bag and keep it dry. I sat down on the aisle seat, knowing that the rain would stop as soon as I escaped it—which it did. Lerner rolled up the flap and tied it with a string that hung from the top of the opening. The countryside began to sparkle as the sun brightened the reds, rusts, yellows, and greens, making the view even more beautiful than before.

The hot, moist air reminded me that I still wore my raincoat.

I took it off, folded it up, and stuffed it into its small pouch, to the amusement of a white-bearded, blue-turbaned man sitting across the aisle from me. My clothes were wet from the rain and from perspiration—the trouble with that plastic raincoat was that it made you sweat so much you were better off not wearing it at all. I had an idea that the man with the white beard understood this. He leaned toward me when our eyes met and said one word:

"American?"

"Yes," I said.

He leaned back with a smile that summed up his opinion of American ingenuity. In this case, he was right and I never wore the thing again; I found that it was no problem drying off after getting wet in an Indian rainstorm. The sun took care of everything.

Eventually, we arrived in Kottayam, a town of 20,000 people on the backwaters of the Arabian Sea. We came in on a bustling street that had no sidewalk. It was noisy, dirty, and crowded. Since the bus now moved ahead very slowly, it was easier to see the people.

Poor as it was, there had been something graceful about the countryside; Kottayam was less poor, perhaps, but it was a frantic place. Tiny box-like open-air shops were crowded together on both sides of the street. They had cloth, tobacco, fruit, jewelry, groceries, and sweets for sale, but no one seemed to be buying anything. Crowds simply surged up and down the street, buying nothing, going nowhere, just walking around on a Sunday morning.

The bus jolted to a stop at the depot. Under a portico, leaning against the pillars, there were a dozen porters in striped vests and *dhotis*. When they saw Lerner and me, they swarmed around us like the beggars in that small town back down the road. They ignored the Indian passengers until it was decided which of them would take our baggage. I appointed one man; he immediately hired three of his pals to help. One man scurried up to the top of the bus and tossed over our two heavy suitcases—a mouldy tarpaulin had kept them dry through the downpour. Before we knew it, everything had been stacked in a waiting rickshaw. A second rickshaw man pulled up, signalling us to get in.

I did not want to ride in anything pulled by a man. I felt no outrage when I saw a scrawny little man pulling a rickshaw with two or three Indians sitting high up on the seat behind him. But, I thought, how would it look for an American to ride the same way? Then it occurred to me that this particularly emaciated and weary-looking rickshaw man was more in need of the rupee I could give him than America was in need of what small good will I might gain for refusing to ride. "How *should* an American act?" I wondered.

Lerner settled the issue for me. "We'll walk," he said.

The rickshaw man grumbled and pulled away.

By now, a crowd of curious children was hanging around us like flies around a sugar bowl. Behind them, I saw the tall man with the gold collar button who had spoken to me at the rest stop.

"How do we get to the Traveller's Bungalow?" I asked.

The tall man set down his luggage, took my arm, and very kindly led me into the street where he could point the way most accurately.

"A furlong down the street," he said, "on the edge of Kottayam."

I thanked him and offered to shake hands. Instead, he gently put his palms and fingers together, the way some Americans pray, holding them beneath his chin and said: "*Namesthe* (nam-e-stay)." It was the lovely Indian sign for greetings and farewells and implied a blessing on me.

I had my typewriter in one hand, but somehow I got both hands up to my chin and replied, "*Namesthe*," with the typewriter dangling from one thumb. I told the rickshaw man with our luggage that we wanted to go to the Traveller's Bungalow; he saluted happily, palm out, with snap and verve, like Gunga Din.

On that last "furlong" before joining up with Project India, we passed a morose-looking Indian sitting behind the counter of a tiny newsstand at the side of the road. His lips were stained bright red from chewing betel nut. In his magazine racks, two picture magazines were prominently displayed: *New China* and *Soviet Russia*. They were printed in English, rather than Malayalam, which is the language of the Travancore-Cochin state, but anyone could look at the pictures and understand their meaning.

Travancore-Cochin state was often described as "fertile ground" for Communist activity. The state has a high literacy rate and an equally high rate of unemployment among the literate. Asian Communists have done some of their most effective recruiting from among such groups. In the 1952 Indian General Elections, the Communists were banned from the ballot in Travancore-Cochin, but they ran as "independents" and won several important offices. Sooner or later, I thought, Project India must meet up with them.

We reached a fork in the road, still trailed by a few curious street boys. The right fork was a shale road leading to a small block of low buildings, all white with red tile roofing which was half-overgrown with green moss. This was the Traveller's Bungalow ("T.B."), India's government-owned equivalent of the American motel, only much older and more accustomed to guests who stay for a week rather than overnight. Each T.B. had its own permanent manager and a staff which prepared food and kept the rooms clean. There were no sheets or blankets, so no one had to make beds. Charges for room and board were $2.50 (twelve rupees) a day. It was always worth at least that much, but sometimes not much more.

Lerner and I had traveled 11,000 miles from New York City to get to this place and begin our story. Quickly, we walked up the drive, hoping we would soon see a familiar face. Before we reached the veranda, two excited California students came bouncing out of the T.B. to welcome us—Rosemary Wooldridge and Joe Michels.

2 ROSEMARY WOOLDRIDGE WAS AN APPLE-CHEEKED GIRL WITH CURLY BROWN HAIR AND A BOYISH FIGURE. SHE WAS TWENTY YEARS OLD. A DEVOUT ROMAN CATHOLIC, ROSE-mary was somewhat strait-laced, but she grabbed my hand and let out her reckless, booming laugh. In a way, her laugh was her surprise.

Rosemary's father was a retired police sergeant (twenty-seven years on the Los Angeles force) and her mother sold real estate. In 1957, Rosemary would get her degree in mathematics and become a schoolteacher. On the U.C.L.A. campus, she was a member of a sorority and engrossed in extra-curricular activities. But when it came to politics, she was one of the two members of Project India who called themselves "non-partisan." The other was Joe Michels.

Joe looked as though he might have been on a vacation. He wore a plaid sport shirt, blue denim trousers, and canvas shoes. His clothes were as light-hearted as Joe himself was serious. He was eighteen years old, the son of a New York executive of Encyclopaedia Britannica, and the youngest member of Project India.

He looked like an all-American sophomore with crew-cut, blond hair, and a build like a blade of grass. He was a fraternity man, played a fair harmonica, and knew a few soft-shoe numbers. But Joe was a philosopher, and at the moment his interest was in the philosophy of pantheism, a religion which he claimed as his own no matter who chuckled at him.

In his excitement over our arrival, Joe stumbled over the corner of my suitcase. He wrung my hand and then wrung Lerner's hand and started to bubble over with news of Project India. We held him off until the luggage had been put up on the veranda and our rickshaw man had been paid.

"Where are the others?" Lerner asked when we sat down on the steps.

"Ed Peck and Ruth Taketaya are sleeping. The rest are at the movies," said Rosemary.

"Movies?"

"They wanted to see the newsreel of Nehru's trip to Russia," Joe said. "I didn't care about going along." Joe liked to sit up all

13

night talking philosophy with a friend, but, to him, two was a large group of people.

Rosemary told us that they had been traveling through Travancore-Cochin state, which was about the size of Connecticut, in a United States Information Service jeep. Along with a driver, the jeep had been lent to them by the U.S.I.S. Librarian in Trivandrum. In two weeks, this Sunday was their first authentic day of rest. Already they had visited eighteen colleges with a total of 6,000 students. From Trivandrum, the capital of the state, they had driven fifty miles to Nagercoil, at the southernmost tip of India, then one hundred miles north to Quilon, Chengannur, and finally Kottayam, where they had arrived the evening before us. In the Kottayam area and the following week in Ernakulam, they would visit fifteen more colleges with a total of 20,000 students. At no time would they be more than ten degrees above the equator.

"Little T-C state," Joe said, "has only three per cent of India's population, but it has forty colleges and over ten per cent of India's college enrollment. A boy with two hundred dollars here can live and get a year of education, but some families don't earn that much in a year."

Joe borrowed a cigarette from me, having long ago run out of American-mades, and Rosemary chided him for mooching. At that point their teammates, Ruth Taketaya and Ed Peck, joined us on the veranda. They were delighted to see us, but they were still half asleep.

Ruth had a severe rash on her hands and in the crook of her elbows—nasty red blisters that seemed to be weeping. Peck had the same kind of rash on the back of his neck. They had eaten mangoes and probably were allergic to this oblong Indian fruit that tastes like a cross between cantaloupe and avocado. A doctor had given them some pills which as yet had not worked on the rashes, merely making the two patients groggy.

Two people with the same rash could hardly have been more different. Ruth, aged twenty-one, had raven hair, black-rimmed glasses, and strong white teeth. She was slight, almost frail, but not a bit afraid of the rash she'd picked up. Like all the members of Project India, excepting Rosemary and Joe, she would graduate from U.C.L.A. in 1956.

During World War II, Ruth was interned with her family at camps for Japanese-Americans, first at Poston, Arizona, and later at notorious Tule Lake, California. Afterwards, the family lived in a house by the side of the Southern Pacific railroad tracks, while Ruth's father worked for the railroad, then for a grape farmer. Finally he saved enough money to start a small chicken farm in San Dimas, not far from Pomona. In high school, Ruth was a straight-A student and won a four year scholarship to U.C.L.A. She studied commercial art. Ruth did not belong to a sorority, but boarded with a family in Los Angeles. She was a Baptist and still a Democrat, in spite of what the government had done to her family during the war.

Ed Peck, for contrast, was a well-built young man with a flat-top haircut, black, bushy eyebrows, and a rugged face. He was twenty-six years old, and the rash made him nervous. "Man, this is the most exciting trip ever," he said to me, reassuring himself.

"Better than the paratroops?"

"Easily," said Ed.

Peck had enlisted in the Army at seventeen. He was an officer at eighteen, with a troop of eight hundred Negro soldiers in his command. Discharged in 1949, he was recalled in 1951. He requested the paratroops, made twenty-two jumps, but did not go overseas. He was discharged for a second time in 1953. Peck was an old-fashioned college boy, even though he was old for it: he had the college spirit, loved beer parties and quartet singing, was pinned to a girl, dressed in style, and kept up on the university lingo.

Ed's father was retired from a dry cleaning business in Los Angeles and now, with Mrs. Peck, ran a modest rooming house. They were Russian Orthodox Catholics, but Ed considered himself a Methodist. His study was business administration.

On the train from Bombay to Trivandrum, Peck had been elected student-captain of the team to work with Jaffie as keeper of the schedule and master of ceremonies.

"Wait," Ed said, "until you hear the song we wrote to the tune of 'God Bless America.' It's called 'Beautiful Travancore.'"

"Where do you sing it?" I asked.

"At the colleges," Peck said. "What we've got here is a kind of road show. We've got to visit two and three and sometimes four colleges in a day. Sometimes they're thirty miles apart, so we have to depend upon making a fast, friendly impression. Songs help us in a big way."

Returning from the movie theater, Everett Brandon, Jerry Lewis, and Bob Jaffie came shuffling up the shale road to the T.B. They were dressed for the weather, except that Everett, a tall, lean Negro, twenty-three years old, wore a maroon and white fraternity hat with Kappa Alpha Psi written on it in Greek letters. We shook hands, and I asked about the newsreel.

"You should have seen it," Jaffie said. "Imagine! It's only three weeks after Nehru completed his Russian tour. They have newsreels of it everywhere and a three-hour documentary ready for showing in every big city—all with Indian narrators."

I knew that when Nehru had visited the United States a few years back, it was eighteen months before *our* movie of his visit reached India. Later in the summer, I saw the Nehru-in-Russia newsreel. Over and over, in Moscow, Leningrad, and Stalingrad, it showed Nehru literally mobbed by cheering Russians, or balancing himself straight up in a fast moving car waving to more Russians, or being greeted by men like Bulganin who really knew how to shake hands, not for a few seconds, but for five hundred feet of film. The whole thing neatly fitted the soft line that the Communists were trolling at the time.

Everett Brandon said he wished the United States had something making the rounds of India's movie theaters that would top the Russian newsreel.

Everett was fourteen the first time he set eyes on the United States. He had been born in the Panama Canal Zone where his father was a manager of a government commissary. When his father died, Everett's mother brought her family to the United States, ultimately settling in Los Angeles where she became a schoolteacher. He went into the Army in 1950, beginning his career in a segregated outfit and ended up as a sergeant in charge of the dispensary at Fort Lewis, Washington, where segregation had been abolished.

Everett transferred to U.C.L.A. from Southern California in February, 1955, joined Kappa Alpha Psi, and was promptly elected president. His fraternity brothers helped him meet Gram's minimum expense money requirement by chipping in one hundred dollars so that he could go to India. An Episcopalian, a Democrat, and a pre-medical student, Everett was a quiet young man—so quiet that I was surprised when he told me he almost made the cheer-leading squad at U.C.L.A.

Jerry Lewis was smaller than Everett, but well-built, with long, carefully combed black hair and a clean, scrubbed look. He was a smiling, patient boy, twenty years old, with a well-to-do Baptist upbringing back of him. His father was a civil engineer and vice-president of a prosperous highway construction company in San Bernardino.

Jerry was a political science major, a Democrat, and wanted to go to a law school after his graduation in 1956. He had been active in campus politics, winning the junior class presidency, but losing the race for president of the student body to a member of Project India, 1954. Jerry had long since given his Theta Delta Chi pin to a girl named Sally Lord and, as it turned out, they were married secretly before Jerry left for India.

It was like Jerry to be the first one to inquire if Lerner and I had our rooms and was everything all right.

"So far no one has showed up to give us a room," I said.

Jerry went inside the bungalow, and returned in a few minutes with Phillip, the manager of the T.B. He was a plump, olive-skinned, middle-aged man, who liked young people. He wore a blue shirt, a *dhoti,* and chaples, which are open sandals held onto the feet by means of single loops around the big toes.

Phillip led us through Project India's bungalow, a three room cottage with two bedrooms separated by a dining room. In one crowded bedroom, Jaffie, Everett, Jerry and Ed slept; in the other bedroom, Ruth, Rosemary, and Joe. All seven beds, after the Indian fashion, were really narrow, low tables, as flat and as hard as anything you've ever pulled a chair up to, covered over with a thin, damp, straw-filled mat that only re-emphasized the hardness beneath it.

Adjoining each bedroom was a "bathroom" with a wash basin and a floor-level toilet. When someone called for water, one of Phillip's helpers would come running in with a full bucket, which was the nearest thing to running water at the T.B.

Lerner and I exchanged rueful glances when we saw the single light bulb in each room, the screenless windows, and the holes in the mosquito netting. We followed Phillip, however, into a courtyard where we could see all four of the T.B buildings at one time, against a background of coconut palms and green shrubs. Three of the buildings were sleeping bungalows, each with a veranda and three or four rooms, but the fourth building was no bigger than a one-car garage. It was the cooking shack, where our meals were prepared over a cowdung-and-wood fire set on a waist-high slab between two hearth stones.

The front bungalow, which we had just left, had been completely occupied by Jaffie and his team. Lerner and I were assigned the largest of four rooms in the central bungalow. The room had two entrances, one of which led directly to a small side porch. It was here that Phillip's staff washed the dishes. The other entrance faced the Project India bungalow, so our room was the common thoroughfare connecting the dishwashing department with the dining room.

Our furnishings were about the same as those we'd seen in the Project India rooms across the court. We had two beds, one mosquito netting, a table, a few chairs, and a ceiling fan. I was never comfortable in that room, and I cannot blame anything but my own upbringing for it. The bed was incredibly hard. The ceiling fan had one speed—cyclonic. It was impossible to lie anywhere in the room without a draft soaring down your neck. With the fan off, the mosquitos zoomed in.

Lerner and I alternated nights sleeping with the mosquito netting. On my off nights, I used a good mosquito dope which kept them from biting, but which did not keep them from making approaches all night, buzzing in frustration.

Phillip, nevertheless, was a most gracious host. He was a good cook, and we got accustomed to the life even if we could not get comfortable.

When we returned from unpacking our things, Jaffie and his six Californians were enjoying the sun, which had come out briefly from among gathering rain clouds. I was thirsty, so I asked Phillip for some boiled water. He brought me a bottle of cool, clear water, which he said he had boiled and filtered. Gram Guenther had put the fear of dysentery into us all, and instinctively I reached for my white halazone pills.

Rosemary had a better pill, a brown one called tethride, which killed all harmful protozoa, including the amoeba of amoebic dysentery.

"It's got iodine in it," she said, "so it discolors the water, but it is better than halazone, which kills everything *except* the amoeba."

"What shall I do with all the halazone I brought with me?" I asked.

"We use that whenever we wouldn't be able to use tethride politely, like at a dinner party. Halazone isn't quite as safe, but it dissolves and becomes invisible," Rosemary said with great solemnity.

On a number of future occasions, when one of us said: "I wonder what became of Sam Halazone," that meant whoever had the little white pills should pass them. It was like belonging to a secret organization; you had to have a stomach developed in Western civilization and know the password.

3 JOE MICHELS AND ED PECK, THE YOUNGEST AND OLDEST MEMBERS OF THE TEAM, ANNOUNCED QUITE SUDDENLY THAT THEY WERE GOING TO HIRE A CAR AND RIDE OVER TO THE next town, Tiruvella, which was eighteen miles south. Lerner and I could come along, they said, but it was private business, and they would not ask the U.S.I.S. jeep driver, a man named Thomas, to run them over.

"It's your money," said Jaffie, who thought they ought to be resting up for the big week ahead, but did not want to say they could not go.

"We've got money," Joe said, a little uncertainly. Renting a car could be expensive.

"I'll pay for it," I said.

"No, we will," said Peck. "It's in a good cause."

"Let *them* pay," said Jaffie, meaning that I should mind my own business.

Bob Lerner transferred his cameras to an inconspicuous Army musette bag and the four of us set off for the center of town, followed by the inevitable half-dozen street boys who always seemed to be lurking or frolicking behind us.

Across from the post office, Ed and Joe found a taxi stand. Three battered, pre-war Chevrolets and their youthful drivers waited calmly there for a fare. When Joe approached them, one curly-haired, bare-footed *taxiwallah* (one who drives a taxi) tossed away the scarlet wad he had been chewing, wiped the red juice from his lips with the corner of his shirt tail, and cleared his throat. Plainly he was the spokesman for the group.

Joe asked confidently: "How much to Tiruvella?"

The spokesman cleared his throat again and shrugged. He did not speak English. Since Joe knew even less of Malayalam, his trip to Tiruvella, for whatever purpose, was ending before it was fairly started. Joe, however, was undaunted.

"Tiruvella! Tiruvella!" he said, pointing south, at the same time jingling all the coins in his pocket. But the sound of his money was no help to the driver; Joe's California accent was beyond comprehension. The man looked amused. He turned to the other drivers, and the three of them began laughing.

A crowd gathered, as always. From it, a serious-looking gentleman stepped forward and courteously offered to translate for Joe and the *taxiwallah*. Through him, a bargain was made. The fellow would take us to Tiruvella, wait one hour, and return us to the T.B. at the rate of twelve annas (about fifteen cents) per mile. Considering the price of gasoline in south India—sixty cents per gallon —the taxi fare seemed to be a bargain, but we learned later that the proper rate was only eight annas (ten cents) per mile.

We reached Tiruvella in an hour. The road had been partly flooded, and we were forced to drive very slowly. Using intricate hand signals, Joe directed the *taxiwallah* to our destination, which was a row of white and red buildings on the crest of a hill. A smooth green lawn lay before us, running the length of the main building and ending abruptly at the edge of a thick palm grove. In the soft light of an overcast sky, the place had the serene atmosphere of a sanitarium.

We had arrived at the Nicholson Syrian School for Girls, at which Jaffie's team had made a brief stop on the way from Chengannur to Kottayam two days before. It had not been a typical visit, since it was not a college, but it was one of the oldest schools in south India and one of the few with a social service program. As we climbed out of the taxi, a delicately handsome, gray-haired woman in a green sari walked over to us. She was Miss Thomas, principal of the school.

"*Namesthe*," she said. "This is a surprise."

"*Namesthe*," we replied.

"I did not expect to see you so soon again," she said.

"*Joe* wanted to come," Ed said.

On this cryptic note, Miss Thomas led us on a path that sloped down and around the main school building to a cluster of smaller buildings. Two of the buildings were made of laterite, the red clay of Malabar, which is cut in wet squares from the ground, dried, and used as cheap bricks.

I caught up with Miss Thomas and learned something about the Nicholson School. It seemed that two Englishwomen had founded it in 1910 to provide a "Christian education" for girls in the vicinity. Beginning at the age of five or six, a girl might board at the school for eleven years, and win a high school diploma. Like most private schools, it was supported by tuitions, fees, and gifts.

Miss Thomas led us into a shaded area that Rousseau might have liked to paint. The grass, the moss, and the palm trees were three distinct shades of green; yellow birds whizzed back and forth between the tile rooftops and the low palm branches. We stopped in front of a laterite bungalow. It was spotlessly clean. This building and the one next to it, Miss Thomas explained, were living quarters for members of the "Little School," which was made up of children from the "depressed classes."

The "Little School," organized in 1927, was an "outlet for service" for the girls of the regular Nicholson School. In it were thirty thin, wide-eyed little girls, aged five to nine. Some were orphans; some were children of itinerant parents who had left them behind temporarily or permanently. They managed their own lives with the guidance of older Nicholson girls and Miss Thomas.

The "Little School" had its own supply of rice and curry stuffs and a crude kitchen in which the children prepared their own food. They mended and washed their own clothes, kept their bungalows clean, and attended special classes where they learned to read and write. When they were able, they could pass into the regular school if there was money available to pay for their food. The sum amounted to two hundred rupees per year (about forty dollars), per child.

When the Project India group had visited the "Little School" on Friday, Ed Peck agreed to "adopt" one of the little girls. He promised to send two hundred rupees from the United States to Miss Thomas for the girl that had impressed him most whenever she became eligible to enter the regular school. Joe Michels had come back to Tiruvella so that he might "adopt" one of the little girls in the same way.

Miss Thomas assembled about fifteen of the girls. Wearing faded clean blouses and long skirts, they hung their heads shyly and looked as though they might run away and hide. Their arms and legs were like twigs. Peck's protege was not among them— she had gone off somewhere for the day. Joe pointed to a girl who was holding her hands tightly clasped beneath her chin.

With her right foot, she was standing on her left foot. "What is her name?" Joe asked.

"Her name is Leela," Miss Thomas said. "She is eight."

Then Miss Thomas spoke softly to Leela in Malayalam. When the child did not move, she spoke more sharply and the little figure moved forward, eyes down, with her hands still tightly clasped. Joe towered over her, like Gulliver. She tried to hide herself behind the end girl, but she was pushed forward. The other girls giggled.

"Tell her I won't hurt her," Joe said, earnestly.

Miss Thomas spoke, and Leela lifted her eyes for half-a-second, then looked at her feet again. She was terrified, and Joe was nervous. Miss Thomas took Leela's hand and led her down the path, with Joe close behind. They took a spur to the left and came to a stop by a moss-covered well. Through Miss Thomas, Joe tried hard to make conversation with Leela, but nothing he could say would reassure her. Finally, he gave up talking and tried to make her laugh. He got down on his haunches, held her hands, and made funny faces. He tried very hard, and just when he was about to admit defeat, Leela laughed out loud. Soon they were walking hand in hand, with Miss Thomas bringing up the rear, and they carried on happily until it was time for us to return to Kottayam.

"She's for me," Joe said with a relieved smile on his face. Giving the two hundred rupees would not have meant anything to him if he had been unable to make Leela laugh. He told Miss Thomas that he would send the money unless he heard from her that Leela was no longer at the "Little School."

Joe pressed his palms and fingers together in farewell and received an answering sign from Leela. Then fashioning the Indian custom to fit the American idiom, as he often did, he turned to the other girls and cried, "*Namesthe,* all!"

When we returned to the T.B., it was night and dinner was on the table. The dining room was rectangular, allowing just enough room for the waiters—or bearers, as they are called—to serve us individually. Our table was long and narrow and covered with an unbleached cotton tablecloth that lasted the whole week we were in Kottayam. On the last day, it looked like a busboy's apron, but the other appointments—dishes, glassware, and silver—were always clean. In my spoon I found the purple vitamin pill which Jaffie provided each day. (On Monday and Thursday he also provided malaria pills.) When all of us were seated, Rosemary said grace.

Phillip's first dinner menu was not his best—thin soup, cold fish, cold meat, cold pudding, and lukewarm tea. He stood beneath the one bare bulb that hung back of our table, and his face saddened as he noticed our lack of enthusiasm. Plates went back to the dishwasher as full as when they came out of the cooking shack. A muscle flickered in Phillip's jaw as he silently vowed never to let such a thing happen again. And it did not, but this first night it was enough to put us in a receptive mood when a strange fat man came in out of the darkness and invited us to have dinner with *him* the very next night. Phillip urged us to accept—evidently, he wished to buy a little time for reorganizing his kitchen; he simply was not prepared to serve bland foods to so many people at one time.

The fat man wore a full-length white gown. His only ornament was a gold stud. His belly was round and full and jiggled when he laughed. With a white beard and a bag of toys, he would have made a first-rate Santa Claus. He had appeared when the pudding was served, and, with Phillip's help as interpreter, he got his message across.

He was K. M. Thomas, owner of the Gomathy Motor Company, which operated a bus service and auto repair shop in Kottayam. According to Phillip, he was one of the wealthiest men in town and wanted to welcome us to Kottayam with a dinner the following evening.

Ed Peck pulled his notebook from his shirt pocket, consulted his schedule, and announced that the evening was free. But he did not want to commit himself or the team to any unnecessary hazards, so his eyes searched Jaffie's face for an answer. For a moment, Jaffie sat very still, a stern look on his face, then he smiled brightly and said, "Of course, we'll go."

Mr. Thomas was overjoyed. In English and Malayalam, he

attempted to describe the glories of his wife's cooking. Then he shook hands all around and vanished. Jaffie was still smiling, and none could tell from the look in his eye whether he believed Mrs. Thomas could really cook.

PART 2 *Next Week, Cochin*

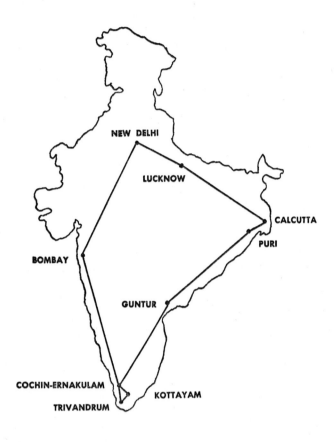

ROUTE OF THE SOUTHERN TEAM

4
clean-looking in their freshly laundered clothes. The laundryman
(*dhobi*) had taken their dirty things, pounded them clean on a
rock, dried them, starched them, and ironed them all in the thirty-
six hours since they had been in Kottayam. With no mechanical
equipment, this was quite a feat.

The manager of the T.B., Phillip, served us a fine breakfast
—fresh fruit, oatmeal, ducks' eggs, toast and tea, the latter in
unlimited quantities. While we were having our second cup, a
young Indian named Thankachou appeared on the veranda. He
was a high school journalist from Pollinatayill-Kayamkillam, a
town somewhat smaller than its name, seventy-five miles south
of Kottayam. He was a frail boy, not more than sixteen years
old, and he spoke very little English. He had come all this distance
merely to chat with the Project India students because he had
read about them in his hometown newspaper.

Everett Brandon joined Thankachou on the veranda. Patiently,
they tried to break the language barrier that separated them.
Thankachou, however, was overwhelmed by the fact that Everett,
a Negro, was part of an American group, and he rather enjoyed
the sound of Everett's voice even if he could not understand what
he was saying. In exchanging ideas, they made little progress.

Jerry Lewis, whose long black hair was as neatly combed as
ever, smiled at me.

"Most of the Indian students seem to like us," he said, "but
we've had our share of angry ones, too, mainly because we've said
something that wasn't *sensitive* enough. I remember one boy last
week handed me his autograph book. I wrote something in it,
signed my name, and passed it back to him. I wanted to apologize
for my poor handwriting, so I smiled at him and I said, 'I hope
you can read this.'"

Jerry demonstrated the act of passing an autograph book in
pantomime. (Collecting autographs is a favorite pastime in India,
as it is in America, but the Indians were more democratic about
it. Almost any stranger in south India rates a page in an auto-

graph book, and Project India names were especially desirable. Even I was asked for my signature from time to time.)

Jerry continued: "The boy took the autograph book from me and, very angrily, he said, '*I can read English, you know!*'"

Jerry whistled and shook his head as if to say the experience had given him a serious, eye-opening jolt. He stood up then and joined Everett Brandon and Thankachou on the veranda. As a student political leader back at U.C.L.A., Jerry had developed qualities of patience, tact, and cheerfulness that made him the most efficient conversationalist on the team; he was prepared to spend the morning chatting with young Thankachou even though only one word in twenty was understood on either side.

When he'd gone, Ed Peck, captain of the team, said: "The thing that really opened my eyes was an incident in an elevator in Bombay when both teams were still together. Sandy Ragins, who now is captain of the Calcutta team, was standing next to an Indian, admiring his sandals. He said, 'Those are nice-looking sandals,' but the Indian did not say anything, and Sandy thought he didn't understand. So he said, 'Shoes! Shoes!' and made an admiring face."

Ed made a funny, rather than admiring, face, but I got the point. He said: "Right away the Indian got the *wrong* idea and said, '*Yes, I am poor and I have no real shoes.*'

"Well, it showed us that some Indians can be pretty thin-skinned about a lot of things, like any new nation, I suppose. But that is what is so exciting about this place. I mean, they speak English like we do so we can talk to them, but otherwise we're so very different. They go barefooted. How can you tell an American back home that it isn't bad to go barefooted?"

Just then, we heard the sound of a drum and a bell, rolling and ringing, very loud and very fast. We ran outside to the retaining wall in front of the T.B. We saw two somber-faced young men marching up the highway. One wore a red turban and carried a snare drum; the other wore a red shirt and staggered under a huge placard advertising the new movie at the local theater. With his free hand, the man with the sign rang a heavy bell; no advertising man ever looked more haggard. When they drew abreast, our eyes were met by those of a sleepy-eyed Indian movie queen, a four-color cardboard replica of the real thing. She was starring in a Malayalam film made in Bombay.

"Oh, boy," said Ruth Taketaya. "Just like our movies."

It did make you wonder why so many bad American pictures were sent to India when it was obvious that the Indians made enough bad ones for themselves.

The California students had the morning off (except for Everett and Jerry who had taken on the responsibility of Thankachou), but that afternoon, Bob Lerner and I saw them in action for the first time. At two o'clock the U.S.I.S. jeep arrived, followed by the same taxi we had chartered for our drive to Tiruvella. Thomas, the jeep driver, was small and wiry with a delicately-bridged nose and a neat mustache. His skin was dark, and he wore a well-pressed khaki fatigue suit with long trousers and a four-pocket jacket.

Thomas was a quiet, careful, bi-lingual man who drove a car skillfully, advised us shrewdly on many practical matters, and was swift in bargaining and interpreting for us. He was able, for instance, to hire the taxi for us at the proper rate of ten cents per mile.

Everyone said good-by to Thankachou, who was returning to Pollinatayill-Kayamkillam that afternoon, and we drove off in a cloud of flying shale. We did not see Thankachou again—until the following week, more than one hundred miles from his home, when he arrived at Project India's Traveller's Bungalow in Ernakulam-Cochin. He came for the same informal purpose and with the same limited result. Finally, I think, Thankachou went home for good.

On the other side of Kottayam, at the edge of town, the jeep pulled up to a large U-shaped building, which was the Christian Missionary Society College, a school for boys and girls, aged sixteen to twenty-one. It combined an intermediary school (akin to our junior college) with a regular four-year college. The place was made of rock and cement, covered with plaster and whitewashed. A portico ran around the U-shape, so that on rainy days the students could go from classroom to classroom without getting wet. Next door was a Jacobite Christian Church, and a huge brown cow grazed there in the dooryard.

The college principal, Mr. P. C. Joseph, a small gray man in a white gown that billowed in the rising monsoon wind, met us and politely explained that rather than call an assembly of the entire institution (the way most college principals in south India had done and would do), he had arranged for each of the California boys to visit a separate classroom. Rosemary and Ruth together were to meet with a girls' class in English literature.

Bob Lerner and I trailed along with Jerry Lewis, who was led into a well-lit, white-walled classroom full of young men in *dhotis*. They were students of history and politics. They sat on long benches behind parallel rows of desks. Every one of them was barefooted. When Jerry introduced himself, many of them laughed, and he had to explain that he was not Jerry Lewis, the movie comedian.

Each member of Project India had a prepared, five-minute opening speech that always could be shortened to as little as one minute in an emergency. The speeches had been written in California and had been perfected along the way, to be presented regularly as a kind of formal, yet individual, introduction for each member of the team.

Jerry Lewis gave his opening speech every time as though he were giving it for the first time. He never failed to get a laugh when he said that his mother was a Democrat and his father was a Republican. This was something new to the students in whose families, whether matriarchal or patriarchal, the head of the family was boss. Jerry explained that he was very much interested in politics, but he stressed the fact that American students paid little attention to the national parties; their emphasis was on campus political life.

Jerry knew, of course, that this emphasis was very different from the Indian students'. They thrived on national party politics. Discouraged from establishing student governments, they had no other outlet. Only a few years ago they had been called by Gandhi and Nehru to help throw off the British yoke—after that, how could anyone get excited about a student council election? They much preferred marching in the streets protesting, say, Pakistan's position on Kashmir, to demanding their own right to a student government—or to taking over responsibility for social problems in their own communities.

The Indian students, therefore, were fascinated by Jerry's talk about U.C.L.A. political affairs, but it must have sounded somewhat tame to most of them. At the end of the five minute speech, Jerry asked for questions. For a full minute they sat smiling at him while he smiled back. Then a boy in the back of the room raised his hand and asked a question that, as far as he was concerned, had nothing to do with Jerry's politics:

"Will you please discuss the Negro question in America?"

It was probably the fiftieth time that Jerry had been asked this same question, but he answered it earnestly, as if it were a new topic.

"There are sixteen million Negro Americans. Their total yearly income is eighty five hundred crore rupees, seventeen billion dollars, the same as Canada whose population is about the same."

The answer was consciously materialistic, but it jolted the Indian students, who were as concerned about material things as anyone else. Some of them quickly figured the annual *per capita* income of Negroes—5,000 rupees ($1,000)—and compared it with the same statistic for all Indians—275 rupees ($55)—expressing their astonishment in low whistles and boyish seat-squirming. As an American, I thought Jerry's answer left much to be desired, but as an American in India I thought it was just about right.

He could have acknowledged racial discrimination in the United States—as Everett Brandon did when I heard him answer the same question later on in the week. He could have properly pointed out that there had been substantial improvement in American race relations since World War II—as Everett did. Then, too, he could have thrown the question back at the students with, "What about *your* caste system?" because, obviously, neither country has a monopoly on discrimination: ours is anthropological, theirs is genetic, and both are equally ugly.

Given the time, the place, and the conflicting information that

Russians, Chinese, Indians, English, and Americans had poured into the heads of these students, Jerry's answer had the best chance of leaving an impression closest to the truth. At least it corrected the widespread, erroneous impression that there were only a few hundred thousand Negroes in the United States altogether, and it proved that these Negroes did not live in a state of extreme depression.

The "Negro question" broke the ice and all at once the air was filled with thin, brown hands waving at the California student. Jerry took the questions one at a time, usually speaking with one hand on his hip and the other gesturing emphatically.

Question: Why are you experimenting with atoms?

Lewis: I'm not a scientist, but I think we're hoping to find peaceful uses for the atom. And I hope India, too, has good luck with its own atomic reactor research now in progress.

Question: Why do you fear Russia?

Lewis: I'm not afraid of Russia.

Question: Well, why don't you disarm?

Lewis: One-sided disarmament is no better today than when Germany was on the march.

Question: Why not let New China join the United Nations? [None of the Indian students ever called it Red China.]

Lewis: I hope Red China will earn admittance someday. Right now they're holding American soldiers and civilians as prisoners. They'll never make it that way.

Question: What do you think of Mr. Truman?

Lewis: I believe that he was sincere but that Franklin D. Roosevelt's shoes were too big for him.

This produced muffled laughter in the audience. Taking advantage of the lull, Lerner and I tip-toed out of the classroom to see what Rosemary and Ruth were up to in their session with the C.M.S. College coeds. The girls had been talking about the kind of songs American college students liked to sing. Their example was "You Are My Sunshine." Midway, when they had sung the line,

Please don't take my sunshine away,

the rain that had been threatening all afternoon came down so hard their voices were lost in the uproar.

Somewhere in the college a bell rang, and the class was dismissed. The students flooded into the corridor, engulfing Jaffie, his team, Lerner, and me, swirling around us, drawing first one and then another into a separate whirlpool. We were crushed together like subway riders; and, even so, students in the rear kept pushing closer and closer to get a word or an autograph book in edgewise, pushing so hard that boys on the outside fell off the porch into the rain. The Indian students passionately wanted to talk to us face-to-face about politics, religion, economics, sex, and school life. They wanted to know what we thought of Nehru, the Immaculate Conception, the price of tapioca, petting parties, and master's degrees. And while we talked, the Indian boys held our hands, which is their custom. Only Lerner escaped because he had a camera in each hand!

The principal, Mr. Joseph, came through the crowd at last and led us away to a faculty tea in the biology laboratory. It was a long, narrow room lined with bottles and tubes, and smelling of formaldehyde, boiled tea, and tangerines. The faculty, about forty men and women—including two Canadians and an Englishman—was poised as one man for our entrance. Rosemary and Ruth entered first, followed by Ed, Joe, Everett, Jerry, and Jaffie. The idea was to get a cup of tea and then find a faculty member to talk with. The Californians carried it off like troops deploying for battle, Rosemary seeking a woman teacher, Ed an economics professor, Joe a philosophy teacher, and the rest taking pot-luck. I carried my cup of tea over to Mr. Backshaw, the lone Englishman.

Backshaw was at least six feet, four inches tall, a sandy-haired man with a thin, bony face and an exhausted sag to his long body. He'd been born in the motherland some forty-five years ago (I judged) and had been teaching English literature in India for twenty years, spending most of his time "up North" where the language is Telegu. He spoke this fluently and also understood Tamil, Hindi, and Malayalam, all of which are as different as French, Italian, and German.

"Bad situation," said he. "I'm teaching Shakespeare this year, two hours a week for two full semesters. Guess how many plays we'll cover? One, just one! Bad situation here. All the students are coming in now with practically no English language. It's being discouraged in the high schools. So they come here and all they know is Malayalam. And guess what? We teach all our courses in English. And hanging over *both* languages is the government in Delhi—they are determined to have everything printed and taught in Hindi. What a situation!"

Backshaw smoked the American cigarette I had given him down to the nub and loped off to pour himself another cup of tea. When he returned, he said, "This year the play is 'Macbeth.' We'll spend an entire hour translating the meaning of a single line just well enough to get on to the next one. That's education?"

I liked Backshaw, but he was easily the unhappiest non-Indian I met all summer, sad eyed, tired, and without hope for his students. I was beginning to feel pretty bad myself, when Mr. Joseph announced that the C.M.S. College basketball team had challenged Project India to a game and that we would proceed to the field of honor.

The basketball court was made of pulverized shale, which had been thoroughly wetted by the storm just past. About two hundred boys lined one side, standing a few yards back from the edge of the court. Ed Peck was bothered by the rash on the back of his neck, so I went into the game with Everett, Joe, Jerry, and a fifth player, one of the Indian students. At first sight, the teams seemed poorly matched. We had shoes on our feet, and they were barefooted. We had three men who were six feet tall or over (Joe, Everett, and me) and they had none. We came from where *real* basketball was played, and they came from Kottayam.

The referee, dressed in white slacks and a purple shirt, threw the ball up at center and we were off. Barefooted on a slippery court, they outran us, outjumped us, and outplayed us. I heard Jaffie laughing as we pumped up and down from basket to basket, all life a red blur, gasping for air. We lost, 22 to 4, a score greatly appreciated by the majority on the sidelines.

After the game, we made our good-byes. By then, each Project

India student had made a friend or two with whom he was exchanging addresses and promises to write in the fall. Mr. Joseph thanked Jaffie for bringing the group to his college, and Jaffie thanked him for the opportunity. To the roar of "Hip, hip, hooray!" we drove away in jeep and taxi, waving from the windows like visiting politicians. Then we sat back in silence for the ride to the T.B.; it had been an exhausting afternoon.

5 ED PECK, RUTH TAKETAYA, AND EVERETT BRANDON DID NOT FEEL UP TO DINNER AT MR. K. M. THOMAS' HOUSE THAT NIGHT, SO ROSEMARY, JOE, JERRY, JAFFIE, LERNER, AND I faced the unknown without them. Mr. Thomas' chauffeur drove us to his house in a 1950 Pontiac, which had cost our host $4,000, imported new from General Motors. The fat, jolly man was waiting for us on the steps of his big stone bungalow. Backlighting from a fluorescent porch light heightened the effect of his obesity and increased our sense of suspense.

Mr. Thomas led us proudly into his living room. It had a colorful coir rug on the floor, several easy chairs, half-a-dozen lamps, an old Emerson radio, and a sharp, clear mirror over the false mantlepiece. On a low table in front of the sofa, there was an array of beer, whisky, and wine bottles. With great ceremony, Mr. Thomas introduced us to four standing men who had arrived before us. One man was a tea planter. Two were bankers—the manager and secretary respectively of the Orient Central Bank of Kottayam, Ltd. The fourth man was a distributor for Burmah Shell gasoline. Like Mr. Thomas, the tea planter and the bank manager wore affluent-looking white gowns with gold collar studs, and the other pair wore Western-style business suits.

We shook hands, Mr. Thomas made a joyful pronouncement in Malayalam, and the Burmah Shell man translated: "Mr. Thomas says that now all his friends are together under his roof."

There were enough seats for everybody, and we no sooner sat down than two barefooted butlers in starched white uniforms marched in with glasses and toasted cashew nuts. One butler ran back for a bottle opener and ice cubes, while the other one stood ready to fill our orders for either Dutch beer, Scotch whisky, or Portuguese wine.

Now temperance was an obvious imperative for Project India, but social graces required each of the students to sip something at least. They chose beer, except for Rosemary, to whom wine was a more familiar drink. The beer was very cold, having been chilled in Mr. Thomas' American-made refrigerator.

We gathered from Mr. Thomas' limited English and the Burmah Shell man's translations that he had bought his first bus twenty-three years ago. He had named the bus and his bus company after his eldest daughter, Gomathy. As of this evening, Gomathy Motors owned four-and-a-half-crore rupees ($90,000) worth of GM buses, a service station, a garage, and some of the choice bus routes in the area. Mr. Thomas was, in short, a burgher of substance.

The tea planter, Haley Mathews, was a tall ex-soccer-player whose broad shoulders strained at the seams of his white gown. His face was wide and strong-looking except for a slightly under-slung jaw, which gave him the expression of a handsome man about to try swallowing his nose. Mathews owned one of the larger tea plantations of south India in the Ghat Mountains east of Kottayam. He did not look forty-five years old, but he claimed that his first name—Haley—was bestowed upon him because Halley's Comet came by the day he was born. That would have been May, 1910, and even though Mathews looked years younger and spelled his name with only one "l," he stuck by his story.

India's forthcoming national prohibition law was on Mathews's mind. It brought a frown to his smooth brow and touched him in his heart of hearts. "Prohibition is all right for the common man," he said, "but for people who can afford it—bootlegging will become a cottage industry."

We heard muffled laughter in the next room which heralded the entrance, at last, of Mrs. Thomas, who came into our presence sideways, pushed forward by two young men. Her husband grandly gestured toward her and said, "This is my wife, mother of my eleven children." Mrs. Thomas blushed and disappeared, never to be seen again, except dimly in the kitchen during dinner.

Haley Mathews described a certain game sanctuary on Periyar Lake in the Ghat Mountains, not far from his own plantation and only a morning's drive from Kottayam. He said that we could see wild elephants, tigers, bison, and strange new birds there if we would only take off one day to visit the place. Mr. Thomas agreed with Mathews. He could not see why Project India spent so much time visiting colleges: "After you've seen one, you've seen them all," he said.

Mathews continued, urging us to be his guests on, say, Saturday for a trip to Periyar Lake. Project India was supposed to drive to

Ernakulam on that day, settle in the Traveller's Bungalow there, and rest until Monday when another round of college visits would begin. The trip to Periyar would mean only that the day of rest was lost, and, of course, all of us were willing to lose it.

Jaffie agreed to the Saturday excursion, and Haley Mathews smiled and kept smiling for the next three hours, he was that happy.

Mr. Thomas arose and led us through a short hallway into the dining room, a long, clean room with fluorescent lights and one long table with eleven card-table chairs. The bare, cement floor was still damp from a recent scrubbing. The table was covered with a blue oil cloth and set for a banquet.

During the next three hours, while Haley Mathews smiled and Mr. Thomas giggled, sixteen different courses were served. The butlers served soup, delicious broth in exquisite china bowls, followed by fish patties, which had been fried, dried, and gently reheated. The plates were cleared, clean ones were set before us, and a second fish course was served, with cold, cooked vegetables on the side.

Then came rice and curried vegetables in a somewhat fluid state; all eyes were turned to the bank secretary who had been eating with his fingers. Nimbly, he formed balls of rice, dipped them in curry, and lobbed them into his mouth without even dirtying the palm of his hand. He paused to explain that eating with one's fingers improves the salivary action, hence aiding digestion and general well-being. We tried the curry ourselves, with forks, happily discovering that it was neither hot nor bitter. There followed several meat dishes, chicken, lamb, and two meats that I could not recognize, more rice, vegetables, and, naturally, endless quantities of Dutch beer, from which Project India abstained.

Every now and then, Mrs. Thomas would peer out from the kitchen to see if we were enjoying ourselves, but it took a fast eye to catch her. It was getting close to midnight when she sent out her masterpiece, a fruit and cream dessert fluffed up and beautifully decorated like a food photograph in a women's magazine.

Haley Mathews produced a leather cigar case, which he passed around after extracting one large green cigar for himself. He lit it and sighed. One could almost hear the music stirring in him. Mathews lifted his voice, a rich, nasal baritone, to sing a Malayalam welcome song, in which he often tripped over his tongue. His near-monotone chant continuously tickled Mr. Thomas and the rest of his friends. They cried for more. It was beginning to look as though we were there for the night.

Rosemary Wooldridge tactfully interrupted. She suggested that the Californians should entertain their hosts and then take their leave.

"This is a song *we* wrote, called 'Beautiful Travancore,'" she said, and Jerry Lewis quickly hummed the proper note. To the tune of "God Bless America," they sang:

> Beautiful Travancore,
> Land of the sun,
> With its palm trees and rice fields,
> Lovely sunsets when long days are done.
> From Cape Cormorin,
> To the mountains
> To the oceans on each side,
> Beautiful Travancore,
> All India's pride.
> Beautiful Travancore
> All India's pride.

There was not a complete sentence to be found in their lyrics, but it was a hit with our Indian friends, just as it was with students all over Travancore-Cochin state. Then, blond Joe Michels, thin as a reed, was moved to demonstrate his loose-jointed soft shoe number to the tune of "By the Light of the Silvery Moon." He had been shy about his dancing prowess earlier in the summer, but by now he was an accomplished and nonchalant hoofer.

The good food, the whirring fan, and the long day which had begun eighteen hours earlier conspired to make the members of Project India sleepy and now seriously anxious to leave. Mr.

Thomas, however, was an indefatigable host. He insisted on serving a nightcap to his guests in the living room. On the way, I caught a glimpse of one of the bedrooms, in which four children were sleeping peacefully under mosquito netting in bunk beds.

On the sofa once again, Haley Mathews was the center of attraction. His eyes were red and his voice thick, but still he smiled—after all he was to be our host on Saturday. I innocently asked him how the tea business was doing these days. The question pulled the cork from his soul. In English and Malayalam, passionately, bitterly, sternly, and at considerable length, he told us that business was terrible. Here he was paying his "coolies" one-rupee-eight-annas (thirty cents) a day, which was twice as much as they got before the war, and yet they complained all the time, were unspeakably lazy, and, goaded by the Communists, they kept asking all the time for higher wages! As suddenly as the flow had started, it stopped, and Haley Mathews merely tossed his head from side to side in disgust.

Jaffie caught the eye of each of us, one by one, and signaled that it definitely was time to leave. We all said, "Namesthe" half a dozen times per person before we finally made our getaway.

On the following Saturday morning, as promised, three cars drove up to our Traveller's Bungalow to take us to the Game Sanctuary at Periyar Lake. At the wheel of the lead car, a '52 Chevrolet, was Haley Mathews himself, while the other two cars were manned by drivers in Mr. Mathews's employ. The only other man we recognized was roly-poly Mr. Thomas of Gomathy Motors, but we soon met our new traveling companions—Haley's brother, Haley's business associate, and Haley's minister—plus the two drivers, who did not speak a word all day. The nine of us made it a party of sixteen.

A few miles outside of Kottayam the road began climbing. During the first hour, we rose 4,000 feet in the Ghats. Monsoon clouds hung on the jungle-green mountaintops, and a cold wind blew through the valleys, unexpected and eerie. Halfway to Periyar Lake, we stopped at a Rest House, a government-sponsored place like the Traveller's Bungalow. The manager was Haley's dear friend and did not protest when Haley unloaded sixteen people at ten o'clock in the morning. Loudly, Haley called for cashew nuts to go with the beer and Scotch whisky his drivers were just unloading from the trunk of his car.

A seventeenth man, a Mr. Chako, met us at the Rest House shortly after our arrival. He turned out to be the Game Warden of Periyar Lake Sanctuary and Haley's very best friend. Chako joined in the morning revelry, while we Americans and the minister hung back as best we could, munching cashews and sipping the warm beer.

Rosemary and Ruth kept smiling valiantly, but once in a while they would show signs of shock. Jaffie and Peck, as leaders, were not happy about the party in the Rest House, but at least the two non-talking drivers were staying strictly out of it. Haley Mathews' ability to drive an automobile, however, was certainly something to worry about. Mathews, meanwhile, was busy describing the elephants and tigers we would see roaming around the Game Sanctuary, while Jerry Lewis, the good listener, nodded appreciatively. Joe Michels, naturally, was in a corner with the reverend, developing a theological point, and Everett stood outside quietly absorbing the wild view. He was wearing his Kappa Alpha Psi hat pulled down tight against the wind.

When it seemed that the Rest House was as close as we were ever going to get to the Periyar sanctuary, Haley abruptly called off this phase of the activities, and we were off again, driving over fifteen miles of treacherous, curving, descending gravel road to the town of Periyar. He would tear over the brief straightaways, brake furiously on the curves, and otherwise maneuver the car like the lead man in the Mexican Road Race.

Ed Peck and I rode with him, his brother, and Chako, the Game Warden. We stopped in Periyar for gas and then raced on through vast acreages of tea trees growing up the steep slopes of the mountains. The gas stop had enabled the two trailing cars to catch up, so we entered the Game Sanctuary together, an American-manufactured auto caravan in a lovely, cool jungle. The air was filled with the chattering alarms of monkeys, and through breaks in the trees we could see the waters of Periyar Lake. In some pre-war year, the British had dammed up hundreds of small mountain streams to create the lake and help control the recurrent floods. And as the British were wont to do, they took advantage of the fruit of their labor by establishing the Game Sanctuary and building Aranya Nivas, the "Forest Lodge," on a suitable bank of the lake. Aranya Nivas was an elegant resort hotel, 3,000 feet above sea level; it had been the ideal getaway place for the Crown's representatives during hot weather.

Now that the British were gone, Aranya Nivas still was ideal for wealthier Indians who spent vacations there in much the same way as the British had done—in comfort, beauty, and plenty. When we arrived, we realized that Haley Mathews had reserved Aranya Nivas for the day. Turbaned servants in semi-military blouses, trousers, and puttees, hustled outside to meet us. We were ushered in through a richly carpeted hall which led to a circular, glassed-in porch, furnished with cushioned bamboo chairs and sofas. It was nearly noon and most of us Americans were hungry, but none of us believed that Haley and the rest could eat without drinking first. It might have been the lunch hour in New York, and the ritual here, as there, required drinks first, food later.

It was not long before singing began, led by Chako, the Game Warden, who knew a great many English songs, including "Clementine," "The Old Oaken Bucket," and of course "Sweet Adeline." Ed Peck, who loved to sing, matched Chako song for song, with the rest of us joining in on the third or fourth bar.

The staff of Aranya Nivas crowded in at the doorway to listen.

Luncheon was served in a sumptuous dining room by eight waiters. It was an elegant meal, surpassing Mr. Thomas' of five nights before. Haley Mathews even cut off the supply of drinks during lunch and we were ready to accept the morning's celebration with great tolerance. We dared hope that Ed Peck and I might get back over the mountain safely even if Mathews drove us at night. But when the party moved down to the lake after lunch, one of the two flat-bottomed launches waiting for us was loaded to the Plimsoll line with a bushel basket of tangerines, a stalk of bananas, fifteen pounds of salted cashew nuts, a case of sparkling water, a case of whisky, and two cases of beer!

Heroically, Lerner and I leapt into the bar-boat and shuffled people around until, in the confusion, Jaffie, the six students, and the reverend wound up in the other boat, while Haley Mathews and his boys were sailing with us and the alcohol, which is where they wanted to be anyhow.

When we set out the lake was smooth, but the sky was grim and threatening. It was a wide lake with the dead tops of drowned trees sticking up in the water a hundred yards from the shore. The trees on land grew right down to the water, but there were wide patches of tall grass through which anything smaller than an elephant might stroll without being seen from the lake. The two launches stayed close together in the beginning, but as the party developed on our boat, we fell back a few yards.

Chako was determined to toast each and every American holiday, beginning with the Fourth of July and ending with Father's Day, after which he began on Indian holidays, of which there are more than one each day if you want to get technical about it, and he did. The wind began to whip up the lake and chill our bones. With our motor chugging fitfully, we sailed for about an hour without seeing any more than a few strange birds, some strange bison drinking at the water's edge, and the laughing faces of our new friends.

Then as the lead boat rounded a grass-covered peninsula, Everett Brandon shouted: "Look, there! A tiger!"

He pointed to the crest of a hill over which a tiger was running with a huge lump of fur in his mouth. The tiger's red-orange, black-striped coat was a gleaming blur as he streaked down the side of the hill through the grass to the water, not thirty feet from the boat. The tiger turned and looked up. A growling brown bear came over the top of the hill determined to rescue the lump of fur—the bear's cub—from the tiger's mouth. Cruelly, the tiger tossed the cub into the lake and prepared to slash up its parent. The cub immediately sank to the bottom and the bear, sensing that there was no longer any reason for fighting, whirled and ran away.

When the second boat arrived, the tiger was frantically searching the shore to find his prize. Mathews and Chako shouted and

screamed wildly to frighten him off. Taking his own sweet time
about it, the tiger moved first one powerful leg and then another
as he moved away. The muscles beneath his loose, sleek coat
worked in slow motion like marvelous pistons. Arrogant and un-
afraid, he began to glide off through the grass, sometimes disap-
pearing in its depths only to reappear a few feet higher up the
hill, until, pausing on the crest, he disappeared for the last time
in one quick movement down the other side.

It was a wondrous sight, and both the Americans and the
Indians felt somehow refreshed, even invigorated.

All the way back to Aranya Nivas rain pelted down, but Haley
Mathews merely ordered the canvas flaps lowered, and we cele-
brated the sight of a wild tiger as the little boat bucked on the
heavy sea. Mr. Thomas offered me a chew of *pan*—betel nut leaf,
tobacco leaf, lime, and arec nut, stuck together with a clove—the
makings for which he kept in an Ex-lax box, but I refused. He
did not understand me, but he smiled and popped a wad into
his own mouth and began chewing merrily.

What all of us needed when we got back to Aranya Nivas was
something hot to drink and, of course, this was precisely what was
waiting for us—hot tea with hot milk on the side and warm
sweets. Haley made his into a hot toddy, and after all the liquor
he had consumed during the afternoon, it seemed imperative to
me that we leave Aranya Nivas as soon as possible so that we
would be as close as we could get to Kottayam before nightfall.
The same thought occurred to Jaffie, who firmly announced that
it was time to leave. About forty-five minutes later we got started.

Lerner and I shook hands gravely, and I climbed into Haley's
car with Ed Peck and Chako. The others rode with the cold-sober,
untalkative drivers, and soon got so far ahead of us that we lost
sight of them. At dusk, Haley stopped at a provisions store, woke
up the proprietor and bought a bottle. Then Chako began singing
risqué songs, and Haley drove like a maniac to catch up. Fog
came in on the night, a fantastic, haunted fog which threw our
headlights back into our eyes and raised up apparitions on both
sides of the narrow road curving through the mountains. Haley
cut his lights and drove on through the darkness, skidding around

hairpin turns, teetering on the edge of sheer cliffs, joyfully following his own instincts and the faint outline of the shoulder illumi-
nated by the irridescent fog.

Long before we reached a source of light, whether it was a
small fire burning before a mountain hovel or the lantern on the
tailgate of a bullock wagon, we would sense its glow in the mist.
And when we would pass by the lights, the hovels and wagons
had a mysterious disembodied quality nearly as frightening as the
insane way Haley Mathews drove his car. Under such pressure,
Ed Peck and I began to sing "Nearer My God to Thee" and "The
Lord's Prayer" with the deepest irony we could muster.

We arrived at the Rest House one hour after the two other cars.
Peck and I were greeted as though we had come back from the
dead. In the light from the single kerosene lamp on the dining
table, we most likely looked more dead than alive.

The manager of the Rest House brought out a hot meal for
every one, and Haley produced the bottle he had bought at the
provisions store. I figured that this must be the last bottle of
whisky, and only a pint bottle at that. If it were *not* drunk by
Haley Mathews, Peck and I might have a chance of getting down
the mountain safely. So I poured myself a waterglassful and managed to waste a few more ounces by spilling some on the table.
I drank about half the glass, gasped, and was about to start on
the second half, when Jaffie came up to me in a state of shock:

"What in God's name are you doing?" he asked me.

"Drinking the whisky," I said.

"But why?"

"So Haley, our pal, cannot."

Jaffie began laughing at me, though I did not think that my ac-
tions were other than courageous, heroic, and beyond the call—
certainly they were not laughable. I even refilled my glass from
Haley's bottle. Jaffie, still overcome with laughter, pointed to the
door through which a member of the Rest House staff was coming
with an armload of bottles just like mine! Fortunately, a few
minutes later Mathews announced that he and Chako were driving back toward Periyar Lake and that Peck and I would be able
to squeeze into the remaining cars. It should not have been a

surprise, because it was easy to see that Haley had become per-turbed by the steadfast temperance of the California students. He was determined to keep on celebrating.

The last we saw of him, he was striding back to the dinner table with his arm around his good friend, the Game Warden, their voices lifted in song. They probably sang all night.

6 ALL THAT WEEK, BETWEEN SUPPER AT MR. THOMAS'
HOUSE AND THE DAY AT PERIYAR LAKE, THE AMERICANS
HAD SEEN LITTLE BESIDES BROWN FACES WITH BLACK
eyes and white teeth staring up at them from auditoriums, classrooms, and playgrounds of colleges in a forty mile radius around
Kottayam. In four days they breezed into ten colleges in six
towns, lecturing, arguing, and listening to the cheers of more
than 7,500 students; drinking gallons of sweet, thick tea; and
singing "Beautiful Travancore," until I, at least, had memorized
the words. As an American, I respected them, precisely because
they were not as good as they might have been.

Within the group, personalities, feuds, and large new ideas
were growing. Rosemary and Ed could not abide Joe Michel's
opening speech and said so, but it was not in Joe to change it.
Gradually, he became somewhat estranged from the rest of the
group and yet continued to do his part effectively. Peck, although
twenty-six years old, had more of the old college spirit in him
than all the rest of the group put together. However, because of
his age he found it difficult to get down to the level of the Indian
students when talking with them in small groups, and his own
feeling of inadequacy prevented him from becoming a strong
group leader.

Everett Brandon, easily the most sensitive person of the lot,
seemed to be approaching a major decision of his own about
himself in relation to white America and at the same time he was
the one who left the most favorable image of America—white
and Negro—in the minds of the Indian students. Jerry Lewis got
to thinking about lifting the sights for his future career, and
Rosemary and Ruth endured the heat, the pace, and the hard
beds better than I would have expected any American girls to
do.

Jaffie had been through all this before. He seemed immune to
the mosquitos, the bitter water, and the small talk of college principals. Day after day he inspired his charges, doctored them,
mothered them, and even played Dutch uncle when the occasion
arose.

There was nothing slick or professional about the group, although during the singing part of their program I thought that Ed Peck acted more like a self-conscious vaudeville performer than a modest college student. Nevertheless, the cheers and friendship they received from the Indian students were uncritical, unquestionably genuine, and aimed at the team as a whole.

One day they drove twenty miles through the rain over back-roads to a small town named Kozencheri. It was a poverty-stricken place surrounded by poverty-stricken villages, in which the people lived just above starvation level. But the college was new, only three years old, and a symbol of hope at least to those who were able to send their sons to it. Room, board, books, and tuition were $250 a year. Built of wood, stone, and white plaster high on a hill and named after St. Thomas, the college had two floors with broad verandas from which there was a sweeping view of the forests and rice fields below.

Backed by a solid mass of students, the principal welcomed the California students and graciously set about showing them the school plant, the laboratories, the classrooms, and the dormitories ("hostels"). In the words of K. M. Thomas of Gomathy Motors, once you have seen a college plant you have seen them all, so the sight-seeing became known as the "Bunsen-burner tour" and was endured rather than enjoyed. Their last stop was the assembly room where the student body, six hundred strong, was waiting patiently for the Americans. Up on the stage, the principal, A. J. Cherian, introduced the troupe, and Ed Peck, as captain of the team, stepped to the rostrum.

"Mr. Cherian, staff, and fellow students—*Namesthe!*" he said, pressing his hands together beneath his chin. The audience roared with delight. It was a good beginning. Very slowly and distinctly, making allowances for the level of English comprehension in the room, Ed continued:

"My name—is—Edward—Peck."

He told them his age and that his family was born in Russia (buzz in the audience). He said that his father came to America penniless forty-five years before and now was retired with enough money for himself and his wife for the rest of their lives. He added some of the details about his own life and then explained what

Project India was all about, his speech being a kind of introduction for the whole program.

Young Joe Michels, following Peck, sauntered forward, set his feet firmly in place like a basketball player getting ready for a free throw, and finally looked at his audience. His shoulders sloped while he held his head high. He was the essence of informality and yet self-conscious and perhaps even a bit afraid. His voice was soft and did not carry well. Joe's speech was based on his own interest in philosophical things, and the substance of it was that all religions are like pearls on a necklace hung around the neck of God. Joe had read all about it in the *Bhaghavad Gita*. From that point on his speech got more complicated and confused, so that by the end of his five minutes, the students were squirming in their seats. But they had seen that an American can be as humanly mixed-up as anyone else.

Ruth Taketaya, frail-looking in her cotton dress, explained that she was an American of Japanese descent, a fact that was incomprehensible to some of the students. Invariably, she would be asked later how things were in Japan these days! Ruth's talk outlined the American educational system, how Americans progressed from grade school to high school to college, and what kind of examinations they were given along the way. It was a compact little speech, but it was not as important as the fact that she, a non-Caucasian, was giving it. In the most out-of-the-way places in India, people know that the United States interned Asiatics during World War II, and Ruth's presence was a kind of unspoken restitution for it. On the other hand, it must be said that south Indians—who are themselves Caucasians—felt more kinship with Africa than the Orient, and for many of the students in the audience, Ruth's racial background held no significance at all.

Rosemary Wooldridge had the good fortune of always being able to give the program a lift merely by saying her name.

"My—name is—Rosemary—Wooldridge," she said, and the young Indians very nearly toppled off their benches laughing. I never understood what was so funny about that name, but it never failed to bring down the house. Rosemary's subject was religion on the campus of U.C.L.A. She emphasized that church and

state were separate in the United States, as in India, and therefore in California. Then she told them about the religious organi-
zations, like the Newman Club for Roman Catholic students and
the University Religious Conference itself, which must function
"off-campus." Rosemary spoke ever so distinctly and clearly, and
her speech was really better than an applause meter would have
indicated. The trouble was that as soon as she finished and the
applause began, Everett Brandon would rise up behind her and
the applause would stop, replaced by excited whispering in the
audience. Often you could hear the word "Negro," sharp and clear
in the uproar.

I have already said that Everett was a quiet boy, but this was
not true when he was on stage. His transformation then was a
delight to behold. Smiling, lean, and handsome, with the Kappa
Alpha Psi cap crammed into his back pocket, Everett reached the
center of the stage in two or three giant strides. Clasping his
hands behind his back, he said:

"My name is Everett Brandon. Since I've been in India, I've
learned that people greet you by saying, 'Namesthe!' Well, in
our country, we just say, 'Hi!'" He raised one hand then and
shouted, "Hi!" The Indian students were too stunned to do more
than laugh.

"Hi!" Everett yelled again.

"Hi!" came the answering roar, followed by cheers, laughter,
and applause—the audience was his, and suddenly the assembly
room was filled with a kind of spontaneous warmth and good will
that only he was able to create. There was a wave of understanding that passed between them—a "colored" audience, a colored
American. It was a very special and wholesome understanding
that is difficult to describe unless you, the reader, happen to be
Jewish, Italian, or Irish, in which case you perhaps know the
feeling.

More than any other American on the team, Everett held in
his hands, his words, and his manner the greatest opportunity to
communicate with the Indians.

Everett first told them that he had been born in the Panama

Above: *The southern team sings a U.C.L.A. song in Alleppey. Left to right are Jerry Lewis, Everett Brandon, Ed Peck, Ruth Taketaya, Joe Michels, and Rosemary Wooldridge. Seated at far left is Bob Jaffie.*

Below: *Near Kottayam, Ed Peck presents a school pennant which bears the motto, "Let there be light."*

Opposite: *Ruth Taketaya and friend share an umbrella in the rain.*

Left: *Everett Brandon and Joe Michels grimly refuse a beggar's pleadings.*

Below: *Smiles are the aftermath of a U.C.L.A. cheer led by Everett Brandon.*

Uproarious students at Union Christian College in Alwaye salute Jerry Lewis.

Rosemary Wooldridge reasons with law students in Ernakulam.

Joe Michels and Leela get ac-
quainted at the "Little School" in
Tiruvella.

Crowd scene around the U.S.I.S.
jeep, typical of Project India's com-
ings and goings in south India.

Boys on the boat dock at Ernakulam.

On the train to Madras, Bob Jaffie writes a letter home.

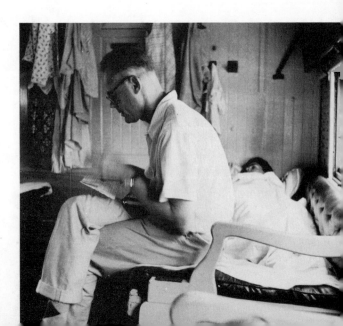

Canal Zone and had come to the United States at the age of fourteen, "Seeing the United States in much the same way as you
would see it for the first time. . . . You would be impressed by
the tall buildings, the subways, the endless fields of crops.
. . . And you would be depressed by the signs in the South that
read 'Whites Only, Negroes Only.' "

Everett paused to look carefully, at his audience. There was
not a sound in the room. Everett continued:

". . . But you would be amazed at the fierce loyalty of our
minorities in spite of these things and at the great strides that
have been made. I am confident that the same spirit that is right-
ing the wrongs in my country will animate itself in all its doings,
both internal and foreign."

His final sentence was a mouthful and a bit of a letdown, but
the Indians seemed to get the idea and cheered him loud and
long.

As in vaudeville, following the stellar attraction is a tough job,
but Jerry Lewis spoke after Everett and usually rose to the occasion, partly because of his never failing, earnest smile and partly
because of his concentration on political affairs.

Taken as a unit, the six speeches were neither brilliant nor
dull, but rather fell somewhere in between. The audience invariably responded enthusiastically. When Jerry finished speaking, the
Indian students themselves were itching to get into the act and
could hardly wait for Ed Peck's next announcement:

"Now, we'll try to answer your questions. Please remember that
we are only students and that we do not represent our government or the opinions of anyone except ourselves."

Questions began to come up from the audience immediately.
Scribbled on sheets of notebook paper or on mere scraps, they
were read first by Peck, who then called up the member of the
team who was best prepared on that particular topic. After these
many days in India, the questions were easily anticipated by
Peck and the rest, but never once did I hear any of them answer
the same question the same way. Not that they changed their
minds every time, but rather, they thought out each question

anew and used new words to express roughly the same answer time and again:

Question: Was the Geneva Summit Conference good for America?

Ruth Taketaya: The conference worked for peace, and peace is good for America and every other nation, too.

Question: What do you think about peaceful coexistence?

Joe Michels: We are coexisting with the Soviet Union now. War is outdated.

Question: What do you think of Nehru's foreign policy?

Ed Peck: I think it is the right foreign policy for India.

Question: What about segregation of Negroes in the United States?

Everett Brandon: The United States isn't infallible, and bad things have been done there, but we have a Constitution and through it we are striving to right the wrongs.

Question: Why have you banned the Communist Party in the United States?

Jerry Lewis: The Communist Party stands for violent world revolution and as such is not within the American idea of changing a government through peaceful means.

Ed Peck: I might add that I feel that as long as the Communist Party stays in Russia and their people put up with it, that's all right, but we don't want it in the United States.

Question: Why are you having the hydrogen bomb?

Everett Brandon: America cannot disarm when other nations are still threatening aggression. My father was wounded in World War I and died a few years later of a cerebral hemorrhage. My brother was wounded in World War II in the Pacific, and I served two years in the Army during the Korean war. I even have another brother in Korea right now. My mother doesn't like to send her family overseas any more than anyone else's mother does.

Question: There is little work here for college-trained people. Is this true in America?

Rosemary Wooldridge: Right now we have very little unemployment in America, and the best jobs are going to people with college training.

SUCH questions were asked over and over, and were answered cordially. Some questions, however, were asked to evoke an obvious answer, in which case a member of the team wriggled out of a definite statement.

Question: Who is contributing most to world peace today? [The answer desired was Nehru, but Ed Peck said only that there are *many* men working for peace.]

Question: What do you think about the Goa situation? [The answer desired was, "India should have it," but Jerry Lewis would only go this far: "Morally it belongs to India, but it should not be taken by force."]

By now, the program was forty-five minutes old, and, like seasoned troupers, the six students stepped to the center of the stage and began to sing. Ed Peck, who had done his share of fraternity-house quartet harmonizing, hummed a note and the sextet belted out the college rouser, "By the Blue Pacific's Rolling Waters," followed by "By the Light of the Silvery Moon," the U.C.L.A. alma mater, and "Beautiful Travancore."

The Indian students were delighted by the rhythm, although I am sure they caught very few of the words. Their applause was only lukewarm until Jerry Lewis separated himself from the sextet by a few yards and sang the first line of the showstopper, a song called "Vio, Vio, Viola."

Jerry: Ich bin der conductor, come from Germanland.
Group: Du bist der conductor, come from Germanland.
Jerry: Ich korn speil-a
Group: Du korn speil-a
Jerry: Auf der viola.
Group: Auf der viola

All (feverishly playing imaginary violas): Vio, vio, viola, viola, vio, vio, viola, vio vio—la! Hey!

The basic verse was repeated over and over, each time substituting a new instrument—a piccolo, a piano, and a tuba—and the appropriate tweet-tweet, plunk-plunk, and oompa-oompa that went with it, ultimately running all together in one intricate finale as in "Old MacDonald's Farm."

Jerry encouraged audience participation—he waved his arms

and said, "Now everybody sing!" many times—but the Indian students were very close to paralysis brought on by an excess of glee. When the song crashed to a finish, the audience went wild, and whatever animosities might have been lingering were dissolved in waves of applause. All was love, to the tune of "Vio, Vio, Viola!"

When everyone had cooled off a little, Ed Peck asked the principal, Mr. Cherian, to stand with him at stage-right. Ed presented him with some picture postcards, which showed scenes of the campus of U.C.L.A. at Westwood. Next he gave Mr. Cherian a 100-rupee note for the St. Thomas College social work activities. The money was part of the fund that had been raised by last year's Project India group. Finally, Ed offered Mr. Cherian a yellow and blue pennant with the university crest and the letters U.C.L.A. inscribed upon it. In measured tones, Ed translated its Latin motto:

"It says, 'Let there be light.'"

Mr. Cherian happily accepted the gifts. Then he announced that while the assembly portion of the program was at an end, each member of the American group would have a separate classroom in which members of the student body would have an opportunity to meet and talk with them. Ed whispered in Mr. Cherian's ear that his friends would like to sing India's national anthem before concluding the assembly; Mr. Cherian's face broke into a smile of wonder and appreciation.

Back in California, the twelve members of Project India had been required to memorize the anthem. The Hindi words were spelled out phonetically for them, and a member of last year's team had taught them the tune. Wherever Project India went, their singing of this particular song at the close of a program never failed to astonish their audiences. This is what they sang:

JANA-GANA-MANA-ADHINAYAKA JAYA HE
BHARATA-BHAGYA-VIDHATA
PUNJABA-SINDHU-GUJARATA-MARATHA-
DRAVIDA-UTKALA-BANGA
VINDHYA-HIMACHALA-YAMUNA-GANGA

UCHCHHALA-JALADHI-TARANGA
TAVA SUBHA NAME JAGE
TAVA SUBHA ASISA MAGE
GAHE TAVA JAYA GATHA
JANA-GANA-MANGAL-DAYAKA JAYA HE
BHARAT BHAGYA VIDHATA
JAYA HE, JAYA HE, JAYA HE,
JAYA JAYA JAYA JAYA HE.

It was a beautiful song, and the fact that the students had troubled themselves to memorize it was deeply appreciated by the Indians. In English the words mean:

Thou art the ruler of the minds of all people, Dispenser of India's destiny. Thy name rouses the hearts of the Punjab, Sind, Gujarat, and Maratha, of the Dravid and Orissa and Bengal; it echoes in the hills of the Vindhyas and the Himalayas, mingles in the music of the Yamuna and the Ganga, and is chanted by the waves of the Indian Sea. They pray for Thy blessings and sing Thy praise. Thou Dispenser of India's destiny. Victory, victory, victory, to Thee!

In a very few minutes, the assembly room cleared, and each of the Americans was given a room in which he or she could hold forth with the Indians at point-blank range. I don't know how Mr. Cherian and the other Indian college principals worked it, but by some magic each of the Americans had a large and attentive audience in the classroom sessions. Everett Brandon, of course, had the biggest audience of all.

Lerner and I shuffled around from room to room, first watching Peck seated on a chair up on a desk talking to sixty or seventy boys who were pressed close before him, then listening to Joe Michels as he sat on the edge of a table and cheerfully mixed his metaphors. We found Everett Brandon a few doors away explaining the art and science of the old college yell to another large group; momentarily, they were more interested in his cheerleading than in race relations in Dixie.

"Now it goes like this, see," Everett shouted. "You say 'U-rah, C-rah, L-rah, A-rah.' Got it? Now let's try it."

The yells of the boys shook the rafters. But Everett was not satisfied.

"Let's go again," he roared, and they banged out the cheer once more. "Okay," Everett said. "Now when I say, 'How is everybody feeling?' you say, 'Satisfied!' "

The Indian boys did not understand. Everett went over it again. "Okay," he said, "How is everybody feeling?"

"Satisfied!"

"Louder!"

"*Satisfied!*"

"How is everybody feeling!"

"SATISFIED!"

"That's great! *Great!*" he said, squeezing the shoulder of the nearest boy and carrying on in this manner until lunch time.

Mr. Cherian had invited the Americans to lunch with him, after which they would push on to another town and another college. But getting away from the schoolyard was difficult because of the milling throng of students. Slowly, we pushed single-file through the crowd. Everett said something to the boys nearest him, and their laughter stopped the whole procession. I was once close enough to overhear one of Everett's remarks. He said: "Sure, I got a girl. I like to kiss her!" The Indian boys were convulsed.

At this point I had an encounter of my own, quite different from Everett's exploits. I had almost arrived at the front steps where Thomas, the U.S.I.S. jeep driver, and the *taxiwallah* were waiting, when an old man wearing a *dhoti* and an academic cowl pulled my sleeve and led me into a deserted classroom. He wore half-glasses, was very near-sighted, and had a brisk manner. Evidently he thought I had been on the stage with the U.C.L.A. students. Quickly, he said:

"I am a teacher here. Do you agree with what your blond young man [Joe] said today, that all religions are alike unto the Lord?"

My inclination was to say, "No," but I thought the man wanted an affirmative answer. There was little time for argument and besides, following the lead of Project India, I felt that I should be as agreeable as possible. So I hedged.

It turned out that the old professor wanted a "No" answer all along. He said: "I do not agree at all, sir. There is but one way. Christ is the Word and the Law." There was fire in his eyes, and for a moment I thought he was going to raise up the crucifix that hung around his neck and ward off my equivocating spirit.

"Well, it is a matter of opinion," I said.

"Your religion, sir?" he asked, quite fiercely.

"Jewish," I said.

This rocked him back on his heels, his glasses skidded down to the end of his nose, and he reached out a crooked, old finger to touch me.

"Now I understand," he said. He probed my chest again with his finger, collected his zeal, and asked: "Do you have *one* thing for me to consider after you've gone?"

It was a passionate challenge, and for a moment, speechless, I was unable to pick up the gauntlet.

"Well, *you* consider *this*, then," he said. *"Jesus is the way."* He pointed that index finger straight up toward heaven.

Suddenly there came into my mind the old Sunday School story of Hillel, who was requested to sum up the essence of Judaism while standing on one foot.

"Do not do unto others that which you would not have them do unto you," I said.

The old man was terribly pleased. We saluted each other with great solemnity, each with palms pressed together before the lips, and he breezed out of the empty classroom, a happy, passionate man.

It had begun to rain outside, and standing alone in the classroom, I felt cold inside. The passion of so many Indians—passion for their many religions, for their languages, for Nehru, for their nation, indeed for us Americans—washes over you like a giant wave and then goes on, leaving behind the feeling that perhaps you are not quite alive enough.

Bob Jaffie interrupted my chilling reverie. Outside they were waiting for me to get in the taxi for the short ride to Mr. Cherian's home. In the driving rain, Indian students still clung to and hugged the U.S.I.S. jeep and shouted through the windows. The drivers eased away from the throng and steered a path through the soaked students who lined the roadway.

Everett stuck his head out of the window to ask how everyone was feeling, and the answer came back, *"Satisfied!"*

7 LIKE A SEASONED TROUPE OF VAUDEVILLEANS, THE CALI-
FORNIA STUDENTS WENT FROM COLLEGE TO COLLEGE IN
THE KOTTAYAM AREA. THEY MADE THEIR SPEECHES, SANG
their songs, answered questions, and moved on at top speed.

At Catholicate College in a town called Pathanamthitta, the
principal could not understand how I could be with Project India
and not be a part of it. He insisted that I join the group up on the
stage. An extra chair was set for me, and I was obliged to occupy
it. From this vantage point, as never before, I felt the adulation
and power that had been offered to the California students at college after college.

The very next day, however, the admiration was on the other
side. The team visited a pair of colleges that shared a single
campus, St. Berchman's College for boys and Assumption College
for girls in the backcountry town of Changanacheri. The girls'
school principal, a tiny, witty, Jacobite nun, warned us that English comprehension at the colleges was low. She exhibited a copy
of the college yearbook printed in English which, unintention-
ally, illustrated her warning.

Under a photograph of a handsome elderly gentleman on the
first page, there was this caption, printed in all seriousness:
"Rt. Rev. Msgr. Sebastian Valloppilly, Apostolic Administrator—
a distinguished old boy."

The girls of Assumption College did not have an assembly room,
but about one hundred and fifty of them had crowded into a classroom on the second floor of their school building. Those who could
not find seats inside were crowded together at the doors and
windows; the ones farthest back were getting damp from a mist
that was gradually becoming rain. Each girl wore her shiny black
hair parted in the middle and braided in a single long pigtail. They
were dressed in green or blue saris, all very soft and fragile-look-
ing.

Because of their unfamiliarity with English, the question-and-
answer period was omitted, but three Indian girls were prepared
to sing for us after the California students concluded their program. A fat girl sang in praise of Gandhi, and a pretty girl sang
and danced an Indian harvest song, which was full of earthy gyra-

tions. While she danced, the rain began to hammer on the roof, and the wind rattled through the wooden shutters.

The last girl, a dark, beautiful child in a blue sari, at first found it difficult to sing above the clamor of the storm. The California students could not hear her first words, but because she stood there transfixed, her eyes looking into space, they thought she must be singing a hymn. Her voice grew, however, and to their utter amazement they realized she was singing an American song—she had learned the words, but had no idea at all what she was singing in such sacred tones:

> Willie, I love you, my darling,
> Love you with all of my heart;
> Tomorrow I might have been married,
> But rambling has kept us apart.
>
> Down through the barroom he staggered
> And fell down by the door;
> The very last words that he uttered,
> "I'll never see brown eyes no more."
>
> Seven long years I've been married,
> I wish I was single again,
> A woman never knows of her troubles
> Until she has married a man.
>
> Beautiful, beautiful brown eyes,
> Beautiful, beautiful brown eyes,
> Beautiful, beautiful brown eyes,
> I'll never love blue eyes again.*

The song had been learned especially for the American students, and nothing in south India so moved and humbled them as this exquisite, honest voice singing those ridiculous words.

At another college that same day, the Nair Service Society

---

* "Beautiful, Beautiful Brown Eyes," written by Arthur Smith and Alston Delmore, Copyrighted American Music, Inc., 1943 and 1951.

College at Changanacheri, the principal kept a student body of nearly 1,500 boys and girls waiting an hour in the assembly room. As a result, the audience was noisy and unruly during most of the presentation. It was Project India's worst afternoon; even Everett could not hold his audience all of the time.

Yet when a certain faculty member, a teacher of history, rose to make a speech, the auditorium became perfectly still. The audience listened carefully to what he had to say and lustily cheered him when he sat down. He had respect, and this is what he said:

"There are two views of the United States in India. One is a noble view. We see America as a broad oak tree whose branches shade all those beneath its leafy limbs.

"The other view is ignoble. Some see America as an octopus whose tentacles squeeze the life out of all who are caught in them.

"It is worth comparing here the Four Freedoms of America's great leader, Franklin Roosevelt, and the famous five points of our own great leader, Pandit Nehru. Mr. Roosevelt said that he sought for all men freedom of speech, freedom of religion, freedom from want, and freedom for fear. Mr. Nehru says that he seeks peace, the liberation of all peoples, the maintenance of freedom, the elimination of discrimination, and the eradication of want, disease, and ignorance.

"From this I would conclude that such differences as we might have are not differences in principle, but rather differences in method, in certain means, rather than in general ends."

By their applause, the Indian students showed that they not only approved the speech, but also liked the Americans—in spite of the reception they had given them. But the history teacher and not the Americans had carried the day. It was a good counterweight for the unqualified affection shown by Indian students elsewhere.

That evening spirits were low, partly from fatigue and partly from this chastening experience. Without enthusiasm, the students kept an appointment to visit the home of the Reverend and Mrs. George Neilsen, a Canadian missionary couple, in Kottayam. It was raining when they arrived at Neilsen's pleasant little bungalow, but every light in the house was turned on, and the place had a feeling of warmth about it even before they were inside.

Reverend Neilsen owned the only Ping-pong table in Kottayam. He had built it himself out of teak-wood, nails, and home-made glue. The boys started a round-robin tournament, which Everett won easily, and for a few hours, at least, they forgot all about India.

Jaffie, Rosemary, and Ruth engaged the Neilsens in a game of Chinese checkers. Our hosts were not full of a lot of questions about Project India; they sensed the Californians' need for escape and did their best to provide it. They even ended the interlude with a pitcher of Kool-Aid and real ice cream, served with cashew nuts, marshmallow sauce, and maple syrup.

As we left, Mr. Neilsen passed out a few booklets for us to read at our leisure. Printed by the Travancore Apostolic Press, the booklets were titled, "Everlasting Punishment!" "What Must I do to Be Saved?" and "Occupy 'Til I Come!" They were filled with the hottest kind of fire and brimstone and were the last thing one would have expected from such a peaceful man.

On the final morning of college visits in the Kottayam area, while riding in the U.S.I.S. jeep, Everett Brandon discussed the line in his speech which said: "You would be depressed by signs in the South that read 'Whites Only, Negroes Only.'" Everett felt that it was the only honest way to discuss discrimination in America.

"I think you're giving the wrong impression," said Rosemary Wooldridge.

"Well, don't I say also that I'm confident America will right its wrongs against the Negroes?" Everett persisted. "Just being here as a part of Project India myself—an American who is not only a Negro but also a pre-medical student—I am proof that democracy can solve its problems."

"But how many Indian students will think of you as proof?" asked Ruth Taketaya, who had a fine ability for getting to the heart of a matter. "They may be too overwhelmed by your presence to add things up."

Everett was in a quandary and didn't know it.

Before he came to India as an unofficial representative of America-as-a-whole, he believed himself to be as much a victim of racial discrimination as any other Negro; he bitterly resented it. Once in India, however, his resentment was overcome by something much more intense—patriotism. Everett began to see himself as an example of what a Negro is able to achieve in "white" America; while discrimination was still painful to him, it had become something that happened to other Negroes—hardly ever to Everett Brandon.

Ruth said: "The Indian students are liable to forget everything else you say—and even forget *you* someday—but they won't forget that the signs read 'Whites Only' down South."

Everett, Rosemary, and Ruth discussed this one sentence in his speech for more than an hour as we drove to Nirmala College, thirty miles east of Kottayam. When he spoke at the college, he changed the key sentence:

". . . and you would be depressed by signs of *discrimination and intolerance,*" he said, and then went on as before, "but you would be amazed at the fierce loyalty of our minorities in spite of these things. . . ."

We heard no more about the "Whites Only" signs.

From Nirmala College, the team drove to the town of Palai, a ramshackle place in the foothills of the Ghat Mountains. The local college again was named for St. Thomas. It was the most elegant building in the neighborhood, and a thousand boys were assembled in its front yard to hear the Americans speak. They let out a great roar as we drove up. The principal cancelled our Bunsen-burner tour in the hope that Project India could get through its program so that the St. Thomas boys could put on *their* program before the inevitable rains came. Briskly, Jaffie and his six troubadours mounted a specially-built platform and began what was their last presentation in the Kottayam area.

The college was three stories high with broad verandas on each floor. Lerner and I, having been frustrated by rain all week long, ran up to the third floor to take some panoramic color pictures of the outdoor scene. By the time we came down to earth again, the American part of the program was over, and an Indian boy had taken the center of the platform for himself. He wore a golden headdress, a jewelled loin cloth, and bells on his ankles. His face was painted green with red circles on his cheeks and heavy black lines over his eyes. Behind him were four conventionally dressed boys.

The boy with the green face stamped his feet, ringing the bells. Then he lifted his arms and began to sing a kind of Malayalam calypso song, called an *ottaenthullal.* The chorus clapped hands and chanted behind him. Warming to his number, he began to improvise verses, adding an English word here and there which referred in a joking way to the visiting Americans. His expression was dead-pan, but what he sang was deliriously funny to the audience and an hilarious mystery to us.

Before he could finish his *ottaenthullal,* the rains descended, and the meeting was adjourned to a room inside the college. Designed to seat perhaps one hundred, the room was soon jam-packed with five times that many people. The boy with the green face continued his merry song. At the close of it, he announced that there would be a slight pause until the next act got underway.

Everett Brandon immediately leapt to his feet and, within sixty seconds, had the room ringing with this cheer:

"T-T-T-H-O! M-M-M-A-S! T-H-O-M-A-S! Thomas! Thomas! *S-A-A-AINT Thomas!*"

The boy with the green face returned, his face washed and his costume exchanged for the usual shirt and *dhoti,* leading six more boys, two of whom carried a *villu,* the strangest musical instrument we had ever seen. It was a combination of a bass fiddle, a drum, and a set of Swiss bells.

Their song was a *villadicham-pattu,* consisting mostly of intricate Malayalam verses enlivened by a great deal of jumping and leaping. It was "rock and roll," Indian-style. We could have watched the *villu* ensemble for hours, but after two songs, the program ended, and we were led into another room for tea with the faculty.

A professor of English enlightened us on the problems of being a schoolteacher in south India:

"We have three major difficulties," he said in a crisp, distinct

English. "Incentive, language, and stability. After a man gets an education he cannot get a job. An Indian with a degree is almost certain to be unemployed or, worse still, forced to take a stupifying job as a filing clerk somewhere. Unemployed intellectuals are often attracted to Communism, and although the Communists are quiescent here now, this has been one of our gravest problems. I'd venture to say that you have yet to have a single incident involving Communists."

The California students had seen a Communist parade in Kottayam, which lasted about three minutes, and had been asked quite a number of questions that seemed Communist-inspired, but aside from that, nothing overt.

"Don't think, however, that the Communists are not with us," the professor went on. "It happens to be politic for them to lay low at the moment. Well, our second big problem is that our language difficulties are increasing. To speak Malayalam at home and in primary and secondary school, which is now the rule, and then come to college where all studies are in English merely adds up to less and less education. And the day may come when you Americans will not be able to go around India the way you do, because we will have lost the English language.

"Finally the problem of teaching is the problem of all forms of work in a young country. India is still far from stable. Think how volatile America was when it was only eight years old. To improve life in India we need foreign help, but like America of one hundred and fifty years ago, we cannot afford foreign entanglements. Yes, we have many problems."

The Indians, we were learning, were often acute in judging their own ills. But a few minutes later the teacher proved that he was less acute in judging the time it would take to cure them. "In another generation," he said, "we will have these problems solved."

It seemed as though it would take much, much longer than that.

Tea was served, after which the principal surprised Jaffie by asking him to speak to the faculty. Somewhere he had gotten the idea that Jaffie was Dean of U.C.L.A. and formally introduced him as such.

"As teachers," Jaffie said, toward the end of his remarks, "you and I share the inherent optimism of teachers. We must and do hope continually that one day a student will receive a spark from us and go on to produce a great idea, a technical advance, a revolution in thinking."

When he sat down again, Jaffie's proteges were applauding as vigorously as the faculty of St. Thomas College. Jaffie, with his resourceful mind and tireless spirit, deepened the new kind of pride they were feeling for their country.

8 TWO DAYS LATER, WE PACKED UP, LEFT THE TRAVELLER'S BUNGALOW IN KOTTAYAM, AND DROVE NORTH TO ERNA-KULAM FOR ANOTHER WEEK OF PROJECT INDIA. COMPARED to Kottayam, Ernakulam was a big city. It was the heart of the Malabar Coast and the major seaport on India's west coast, south of Bombay. The harbor was filled with tankers and merchant ships flying the flags of England, France, Panama, Sweden, and America. Barges and country boats and tiny fishing skiffs were scattered in between.

As soon as we had dropped our luggage at the Ernakulam Travel-ler's Bungalow, Jerry Lewis, Everett Brandon, Lerner, and I strolled down to the sea wall. From where we stood, we could see Wellingdon Island, on which was the national airport and the Malabar Hotel, and the island of Cochin with its twin cities of Fort Cochin and Mattancheri.

Ernakulam was the mainland city, built when Fort Cochin could no longer handle the shipping traffic. It had surpassed its parent in size and importance, but not in beauty. We could see white stone warehouses with yellow and gold roofs built at the water's edge on Cochin, backed by palm trees and the deep blue Arabian Sea. Between Cochin and Ernakulam was the bay whose waters flowed down from Calicut in the north to Cape Cormorin in the south. One could make the journey on a country boat without once venturing out on to open sea.

Further down the sea wall, Everett found a wide canal through which the country boats came to market, bringing fish, fruit, and vegetables to the *ghats* (steps) where they were sold on the spot or carried to the marketplace a hundred yards away. Fishwives—ugly, frail women with nasty tongues—were standing on the *ghats* arguing with the boatmen when we arrived. Everett's appearance on the scene, wearing his plastic raincoat and the Kappa Alpha Psi hat, interrupted a fishwife's harangue probably for the first time in the history of the town.

Awed and self-conscious, the country boatmen and the fishwives and hangers-on gave Everett a shy look as he moved among them, peering into the dark recesses of the boats and examining their wares. A little boy with a pointed felt cap and an elfin smile walked

69

behind Everett and imitated his every move. Soon a second little
boy and a third and fourth, all dressed in rags, thin, barefooted, and
enchanted, began to follow Everett and stayed with him even as
we headed home.

On our return walk to the T.B., we passed through the main
streets of Ernakulam which was much the same as Kottayam's
except that the shops looked more substantial. You could buy cloth
from three open-air shops in a row, provisions from three more, and
chaples and Western-style shoes from another three. At the bookstores you could buy battered American paper-backs as well as
Hindi, Malayalam, and English publications. The only monopolist
in town was a man who sold eye glasses on the street.

Our retinue of urchins had grown by now to more than a dozen
rambunctious children. They had begun to beg for favors—money,
candy, or whatever we had. Cavorting around us, laughing and
pointing, they were determined to conquer us. Everett was the
first to give in. He brought out a fresh roll of Life-Savers. The boys
rioted. They leaped in the air trying to reach Everett's hand,
tumbled over one another, and screeched with joy. When one of
them finally got hold of a Life-Saver, he immediately swallowed it
whole and rejoined the fray. They did not calm down until Everett
shouted, "All gone!" and showed them that his pockets were empty.

Our own lunch was waiting for us when we returned to the
Traveller's Bungalow. The manager, a fat, bald, near-sighted man
who called himself Paul and looked like Zero Mostel, had prepared
for us the first of many sorry meals. The dining room was decorated
with a Malayalam wall map of India and an advertisement for
Love-O-Fruit Tonic. For luncheon music, we had the coarse cawing
of the scavenger crows which infested the backyard and the wet,
slapping noises of a lone *dhobi* (laundryman) who stood by the
well, pounding clothes on a rock.

During the afternoon, Harold Otwell, the United States Information Service Librarian, arrived from Trivandrum by plane. He had
arranged the south India schedule for Project India and was to
spend the week with the team, not to emphasize the association of
the U.S. Government with the project, but rather to observe its

progress. Otwell was thin, with graying hair, a sharp pair of blue
eyes, and a narrow jaw. His manner was very mild, but there was
about him a kind of quiet, amused independence that was reassuring to see in our much abused Foreign Service.

Ed Peck, the captain of the team, reported to Otwell that the
song "Beautiful Travancore" had been an unqualified hit with the
students further south. Otwell replied that the title phrase had
better be changed since the name of the state, Travancore-Cochin,
represented a compromise of jealousies between the southern or
Travancore part and the northern or Cochin part. He suggested the
Malayalam word, "Karala" (land of the coconut palms), whose
meaning encompasses all of Travancore-Cochin state. Indeed, in
the revision of states proposed by Prime Minister Nehru, Karala
would be T.C.'s new name. Thus, Project India's most popular
song became "Beautiful Karala" and was as rhythmic as ever.

Otwell also had a piece of news: "Do you all remember the press
conference this team had in Trivandrum? It turns out that there
was a reporter there from a Malayalam Communist newspaper.
He took down everything Ruth Taketaya said and reported exactly
the *opposite!*"

Otwell smiled when he spoke, but Ruth was frightened.

"Why'd he pick on me?" she asked.

"No reason," Otwell said. "I've assured Delhi the whole thing
is false, that the remarks attributed to Ruth were impossible."

"Well, my God!" Ruth said, in pain.

"It's a closed matter, but something to remember," Otwell concluded.

Neither Ruth nor any of the others could quite believe that a
reporter would misquote them.

HAROLD OTWELL's new schedule for Project India was only slightly
less frantic than the one of the week just ended. On their third
day in Ernakulam, the State University's Law College was on the
agenda. The law students, ranging in age from nineteen to forty,
were expected to present a considerable challenge. (Two years
before, another Project India team had presented itself to the

law students and was mercilessly baited and nagged by a small clique of pro-Communist students.) The walk from the T.B. to the Law College was a mere three blocks, but as the Californians covered the distance they had the indescribable sense of entering the Big Time.

The mock courtroom of the Law College looked like the scene from an English movie about Old Bailey. I half-expected to see a judge wearing a white wig sitting on the bench, but there was only the principal of the Law College, wearing his own hair and a white linen business suit. The six Americans stood in a pit before the judge's bench surrounded on three sides by tiers of oak-paneled desks, behind each of which was a law student. Many wore mustaches and some had beards. They looked down on the Americans with facial expressions varying from intense interest to ennui. In the back row was a handful of female students. Their saris were the only patches of warm color in the dreary big room.

Ed Peck, according to the Project India routine, spoke first. He made his customary gesture and said, "*Namesthe*," but the response was mild now. While Peck talked, I found myself gazing around the room, noticing the bare feet sticking out from under those austere desks. Jaffie smiled at me as if to say, "This will be a good test for them."

Peck spoke again at the end of the speech-making with more than his usual emphasis, reminding the law students that Project India did not represent the United States Government.

Then a heavy-set bearded man of around thirty-five rose in the back of the room to ask: "Why is it that in spite of your prosperity, your crimes are improving." There was a ripple of laughter.

Jerry Lewis said, "There's no doubt that crime is a problem in America as everywhere else, but I don't see that it is increasing out of proportion to our growth in population."

"Why was it necessary to impound your Japanese citizens during World War II?"

Ruth answered: "The government has been trying to make up for it ever since."

"Are you in favor of another war?"

Peck said, "No."

"What do you do at a petting party?"

Jerry Lewis sidestepped: "I don't know, since I haven't been to one."

And so it went. If there were pro-Communist students in the audience, they never peeped. Perhaps, as the professor of English at St. Thomas College in Palai had said, the Communists were laying low this summer. Or perhaps the principal had taken steps to see that there would not be a repetition of the events of two years before. At any rate, the Law College was a letdown; the students were less inquisitive than some of the undergraduates in the back country around Kottayam. It made you wonder about the future leadership of the state.

The assembly broke up into small groups, and it was dusk before the California students were able to leave. The lights of Cochin harbor were on—lanterns in country boats, electric lights seen through the portholes of merchant ships, and the many lights of Fort Cochin and Mattancheri across the bay. Every member of the team knew that the day's big event had been no contest and was disappointed.

Everett and Joe, however, had succeeded in one thing—they had made a friend: a handsome, broad-shouldered law student who wore a shirt and *dhoti* and carried an umbrella. His name was M. C. Allen, but the boys were already calling him Al. He made all kinds of hospitable proposals that would inconvenience himself but would enhance the pleasure of the Americans. Particularly, he wanted to take them to Panbkad, a "real" Indian village situated on an island in the backwaters a few miles from Ernakulam. The next morning's schedule was clear, so the date was made.

9 BEFORE BREAKFAST, M. C. ALLEN, THE HANDSOME LAW STUDENT, CAME BY TO GUIDE US TO PANBKAD. JAFFIE, RUTH, AND ROSEMARY HAD DECIDED NOT TO GO ALONG, BUT THE boys bolted their meal and rushed out to join their new friend. Lerner and I caught up with them at the ferry boat landing.

A ticket on the *St. Rita,* which would ferry us to Panbkad in half an hour, cost two annas (three and a half cents). Our little group sat in the bow and was the center of attraction. Everyone from the first mate to a blind psalm singer came forward to meet us and say a friendly word. We learned that we were the only ones debarking at Panbkad, a place that few people visited and fewer still could afford to leave. According to our guide, Allen, a village may be defined as an inhabited place which is inaccessable by ordinary means of communication. A majority of India's 377,-000,000 people live in such villages. Panbkad did not precisely fit Allen's definition, because it could be reached by water, but inaccessability is a state of mind as well as a physical fact—Panbkad *was* a village.

It was an agricultural community covering an area of three square miles, worked by sharecroppers who had not changed their way of life in hundreds of years. They grew rice and fished for a living. Their land was owned by landlords, mostly *in absentia.* All the coconuts in the palm trees belonged to the landlords, and people were forbidden to climb a tree to pick one. They were not even allowed to gather up coconuts that had fallen to the ground. Coconut poachers were inevitably reported to the landlords by someone anxious to curry favor.

When the ferry touched shore at Panbkad, the backwaters were splashing against the boat-dock. We were not expected, so no one was there to meet us. The whole island seemed deserted. Panbkad did not have a cluster of village homes as one might have expected. Rather, the people lived more or less separately, spread out around the edges of an intricate network of dikes and rice paddies.

We stopped to inspect the inside of a home and chat with a family. The hut was made of palm leaves and strips of wood and had a hard, well-swept dirt floor. There were a few cooking urns neatly stacked in one corner, and a ragged straw mat was rolled up in another. Speaking Malayalam, the mother and her children came out to answer a few of Allen's questions, but the man of the house shyly stayed inside. Since the matriarchal system prevailed in Panbkad, the male of the species was rated only slight higher than a household pet.

Jerry Lewis, whose smile had completely won the lady of the house, said: "They keep their homes so clean!"

A clouded look appeared in Everett Brandon's eyes, but he made no reply.

Single file, we walked along the dikes through the paddies. Looking down, one could see finger prints in the mud and then, with a sweeping glance, realized that all the miles of dikes on Panbkad had been put together a handful of mud at a time. It must have been incredibly hard work.

Word of the visitors on the island somehow had traveled ahead very fast. In one of the central meeting areas of Panbkad—many paths came into a primitive traffic circle here—about thirty women, children, and men gathered expectantly under a giant palm tree. Ed Peck, Joe Michels, Everett Brandon, and Jerry Lewis burst in on them from behind, as the people had been watching for their arrival on another path. Surprised, everyone said "Namesthe" at once.

To one side, there was a small hut with a Malayalam sign over the door. Few people on Panbkad could read the sign, but everyone knew that this was the social worker's hut, in which a young lady from the mainland at intervals conducted a children's class in dancing. The class helped the local people preserve their own culture, which was not thriving on its own these days. Three little girls dressed in faded blouses and ragged skirts stepped from the crowd. They were hardly tall enough to be six-year-olds, but Allen said they were aged ten, at least. "They do not eat very well," he said. "But they have been learning how to dance."

One child sang sweetly, and all three waved their thin little arms and tapped their bare feet. The tempo was slow and delicate, and their movements were like waving rice. They moved in intricate circles until, at the end, they stood absolutely still with their hands above their heads reaching for the sun.

The four boys from America responded to the three little girls by singing pieces from their Project India repertoire. Joe Michels, hands in pockets, even tapped out his drollest soft-shoe number on the soggy ground. His audience liked it.

We walked on. It was about eleven o'clock in the morning, and the sun was beating down unmercifully. We passed several huts which had their own private water supply—a stagnant pool of green water in the front yard. Husbands and sons were sitting just inside the doorways, staring idly into space.

Allen said that at this season of the year the rice needed little attention, and the farmers had nothing but time on their hands.

"It's a problem all over India. They could repair their homes or fix up this and that, but then the women would have nothing to do. So without any other interest or outlet, they loaf. They're bored. It hurts them physically and mentally."

Then we came to the rather elegant residence of the local Hindu priest. An attendant informed us that we, as non-Hindus, could not enter. Allen, who was a Christian, said disdainfully, "All old customs. They all must go."

Ed Peck said that it would take a hundred years.

Allen disagreed: "Two years ago, we could not have come into this man's garden, and now we are at his back door."

A giant coconut palm tree towered above us in the garden. When the priest appeared, we were admiring its fruit and thinking how thirsty we were. As the priest owned this tree, he invited us to a drink of fresh coconut milk. His attendent tied a heavy rope around his ankles, shoved a machete into his waistband, and scurried up the tree. He chopped off six coconuts which came hurtling down like bombs. In a twinkling, the man returned to earth and with great speed and skill peeled a coconut for each of us. The milk was clear, cool, and sweet. We drank deeply, then shared our drink with three village men who had wandered in to watch what was for them a rare sight.

Refreshed, we thanked the priest and walked past his house to the Hindu temple next door. It was a small white stone building with a tile dome. A sexton stood on a line twenty yards from the temple, holding up his hand like a policeman. If we had come any closer, it would have been necessary to clean the temple, smash the icons, and perform many strenuous rituals before the place would be pure again.

The sexton produced one icon, however, for us to admire at a distance. Through Allen, he explained that this was the Goddess of Rain. She was a delicate figure of silver and gold with eight arms and a knowing smile. When the Goddess was returned to the temple, the sexton brought us flowers for our hair and a handful of purple powder which he daubed on our foreheads. It was a *kum-kum* mark, the wearing of which signified that one had visited a Hindu temple.

On our way back to the boat-dock, the noonday heat was intense. Men were bathing now in the stagnant pools in front of their huts, the few people who had been working sections of the rice fields were gone from sight, and for the first time we were aware of the *silence* of Panbkad. Bird calls and the far-off lapping of water were the only sounds, yet they were more akin to the silence and sadness of Panbkad than to any sense of noise and life. We crossed over a trap set into a dike. It was designed to catch whatever fish might swim through when water from one paddy was drained off into another. A minnow was caught in the trap, but it was much too small to make a meal, even on Panbkad. Then, before the ferry arrived, Allen gave his shoes to a Panbkad boy who had followed us most of the morning.

The wind stirred up the waves on our return trip, but the *St. Rita* was a sturdy ship and rolled nicely with each new shock from the water. We passed a heavily-loaded country boat with eight naked oarsmen fighting the unfriendly water, leaning forward with a good grip on their oar-handles, straining back into the wind, and pulling hard and down until they were lying prone at the end of the stroke. Their forearms did not look strong, but for a few powerful seconds they held abreast of the ferry. And as long as they remained in sight, their rhythm remained smooth and enduring.

Blond Joe Michels, the young philosopher, began a serious discussion with a stranger who sat next to him. I caught a few of their words, enough to realize that they were discussing "non-violence."

Joe had a knack for bringing out the philosopher in anyone, and his new friend, a man twice his age, was delighted to find such an adversary on a ferry in the Cochin backwaters. He shook hands vigorously and seemed about to kiss Joe before we were able to extricate him at the ferry landing in Ernakulam.

Jerry, Everett, and Ed were amused by Joe's intellectual conquest, and they were laughing as they walked off the pier with Allen—but their mood was dissolved in an instant by the onslaught of a dozen or more beggars. Cripples, urchins, and blind men plucked at their sleeves as they ran the gauntlet, grimly convinced that it would be wrong to give them any money. Then they were absolutely stopped in their tracks by a man and a baby, without an umbrella or clothing, lying in the street before them, practically cooking in the noonday sun. The man's legs were bent up behind his back and tucked under his arms, which themselves were bent in the shape of chicken wings after the meat is gone. The baby, not more than a year old, lay in the shade of the deformed man's body, too dazed to cry. The man had been deformed *by* someone for the very purpose of beggary, and the baby was an obvious candidate for the same cruel fate. The boys walked on without paying for what they saw, but what they had seen was not easily forgotten. Poor Allen was more shocked than any of them. After all, this was his country.

10 BACK AT THE T.B., EVERETT BRANDON AND I CHATTED IN THE ROOM HE SHARED WITH JOE MICHELS. WE SAT FACING EACH OTHER ON THE EDGES OF THE BEDS. THE MOSQUITO netting was rolled up, and the ceiling fan was spinning lazily. Everett idly twirled in his hands that Kappa Alpha Psi hat.

"I think I'm more sensitive to certain things than the rest of the team," he said, "more sensitive to how these Indian students treat us—how they approach *me* and, say, Joe Michels."

Joe and Everett really looked very much alike. Both were tall and lean with long faces and full lips. The only difference was that Joe was white and Everett was colored.

"When an Indian student approaches Joe," Everett continued, "he sees a white person and feels somehow inferior. At every college an Indian boy has told me that he feels closer to me because I'm colored 'like' him. When I smile, they're delighted to see me smile. When Joe or Jerry smile, I can feel that they are bwildered that a white person can smile like that.

"Out at Panbkad, Allen said to me, 'I think you can feel this the way I do, because in America your people have been oppressed.' The *indignity* of that village—it *does* take a person who has suffered indignity to really feel it. The rest of our boys, they go into a hovel, and they see that the house is clean."

I remembered Everett's face when Jerry Lewis had come out of the hut on the island and said enthusiastically: "They keep their homes so clean!"

"Clean!" Everett said again. "But don't they see that those people have no hope and how difficult their problems are? You see where a baby has to sleep, no chimney for the smoke to get out, how the men lie around with nothing to do. You saw. They can't even climb a tree to get fruit. I don't say I'm more sensitive because I'm a Negro. I just feel these things more, that's all.

"We went into an ivory shop further south. We saw a man using a chisel and holding the piece of ivory between his feet. His feet were all marked and scarred. So one of the team says, 'Isn't it great what that man can do with a chisel!' And I saw only that it is a terrible way to have to work, where your working

79

conditions are so bad that you have to cut your feet to do the job.

"Don't get me wrong," Everett said, dropping his hat and staring at the palms of his hands. "I think the kids on this team are real, real great, but I tell you they know less about the Negro problem in Los Angeles than they know about India!

"I sat up all night our first night in Bombay, looking out the hotel window at the people sleeping in the streets. I was sick that no one feels responsibility for them. I'm sick that so many young Indian kids, regardless of ability, will have no opportunity.

"Here and there we've had lunch at Indian Rotary Clubs. You meet the top people in a town there. They are lavish with their food and with their praise for us—mere visiting college kids. There are many outstanding Indian college students, but the Rotarians wouldn't think of having the same attitude toward their own. Imagine that—the top people! They all wanted us to know that they're trying to keep the beggars out of the streets, but none of them have any feeling for the beggar himself.

"Some people have a feeling though. In spite of what Jerry Lewis said about that clean hut, he has it. He feels."

We started talking about Indian students we had met.

"Some are fine," Everett asserted, "like Allen. But I am disappointed in others—those that go to school with no interest in education other than prestige. We've got students like that in the States, too, but somehow you don't expect that here.

"Then, too, some of the Indians discriminate as much as our people in the deep South. One kid asked me if we colored people should unite to form a colored union of the world. I said to him, 'If you can't be a brother to your neighbor, how can you be a brother to people you've never seen.'

"I get the feeling that some Indian students think they are superior to Americans in one big way—they're *spiritual* while we're so unspiritual and materialistic. That gets me all excited, because I simply haven't seen as much goodness here as I've seen in America."

Everett lay back on his bed, covering his eyes with the hat. I asked him what's to be done about it all. He uncovered his eyes and said:

"The educated people here don't take enough interest in their government. I mean, it seems that someone is pushing reform down from above all the time. They all say they'll work harder and hire fewer servants. They say things are better than they were eight years ago and that they'll be better still eight years from now. Maybe, but I don't know—it still seems that economic development is the great problem. Same thing for the Negroes in America.

"Just compare. At home I'm perfectly satisfied to have my own social life if I could just feel the freedom to have any job I want, if I could reap the benefits of any work I do—Negroes would be very satisfied if they could have these things. Same for India. If students—and all the rest of the people—could just get decent jobs and be free, they'd be satisfied."

In a little while, when I'd returned to my own room, I thought about Everett's last words. It was obvious that when he was leading his most popular cheer—"How is everybody feeling? Satisfied!"—neither he nor his student audiences were being perfectly frank.

It was not difficult to understand Everett's pessimism. It was true that most of the colleges had low scholastic standards, a minimum of educational equipment—from books to soccer balls —and a tradition which discouraged such extra-curricular activities as intercollegiate athletics and part-time jobs for students. An educated Indian's opportunity to "get jobs" and "be satisfied" was curtailed not by prejudice, but by poverty, stodginess, and insecurity.

The very next day, however, Everett's hopes got a boost when the team visited Union Christian College in Alwaye, a town not far from Ernakulam.

As soon as the California students arrived there, they were taken into a compound formed by two long, low, modern-looking buildings. White walls gleamed in the sunlight. About one thousand boys and girls were waiting for Project India, but they greeted them as though they were good friends rather than heroes. The principal divided the throng into three groups and with a modest gesture dispatched each group into separate schoolrooms.

The college had no auditorium, so he had decided to let two Americans talk to each group for twenty minutes and then shift, so that in the course of an hour all of the Indian students would hear all of the Americans.

This worked smoothly, and an hour later, when the formal program had ended, the sun-washed compound was once again filled with orderly young people. Very shortly, Ed Peck, Jerry Lewis, and Everett were leading cheers and singing songs. Rosemary and Ruth, with a hundred girls clustered around them, urged the ones nearest them to join in. Surprisingly, the Indian girls did join in, silencing the Indian boys, who were too stunned by such boldness to go on.

I was standing next to the principal, who said to me: "Your people certainly know how to unbutton our youngsters." He seemed happy about it.

Later the team toured the college plant. It was no ordinary college, and for once the Bunsen-burner tour held their interest. The library, for example, was unlike most they had seen. The books were not under lock and key, and the periodical racks were well-stacked with current magazines and papers. The college athletic facilities were comparable to those of any American college in the 1,000-student class. Boys were playing intra-mural basketball, volleyball, and soccer. Members of the track-and-field team were practicing pole-vaulting and putting the shot. Everett Brandon borrowed a pole and made a respectable vault, while Jerry Lewis tossed the shot with considerable force.

Most of the Union Christian College students, having left the visiting Americans in the compound, were now watching an inter-collegiate field hockey game between their school and St. Albert's College of Ernakulam. One could see how teen-age energies, which troubled so many Indian college authorities, were used up at U.C.C.

The Americans walked on, beyond a group of boys at cricket practice, until they came to a rolling, lumpy field that was being leveled for use as a second field hockey gridiron. Coming closer to the workmen, they suddenly recognized a faculty member who had spoken to them earlier. He was supervising the leveling operation, and his "men" were volunteer U.C.C. students. They were working with their hands—digging, leveling, and hauling with merely a few primitive shovels and wicker baskets. The system of caste which prevented so many educated Indians from hard labor evidently had been broken down at this college. All of us— and especially Everett—watched the boys work, and Ed and Jerry wound up helping to carry dirt away until it was time to return to Ernakulam.

My earlier conversation with Everett Brandon was not mentioned on the way home or that evening, but Everett was in high spirits for the rest of the day. He and Joe even bought *dhotis* in Ernakulam and, with the help of the T.B. manager, put them on and wore them to dinner.

All of us, in fact, were in a gay mood. It had been that kind of an afternoon.

THAT night, I went around to the room shared by Ed Peck and Jerry Lewis. Ed was sitting on the edge of his bed in his undershorts writing a letter to his girl in Los Angeles. Jerry had his shoes off and was lying down contemplating the ceiling. In the center of the room a single light bulb dangled from the end of a cord. It cast a milk-white glow over their faces; they looked tired.

I pulled up the only chair in the room. Soon we were talking about what was often on their minds: how successful are we?

Peck, who was twenty-six years old, said: "Sometimes I feel I'm too old and out of place for this kind of thing. I guess that's why I overdo this college rah-rah stuff. I keep asking myself if we're getting across as well as we should. I keep trying to speak slowly and clearly and make myself understood. But you get casual about it when they cheer you and crowd around. I know we should be more humble. But it's tough to maintain a humble attitude before these very young Indian college kids. Most of them are under twenty and at one school there was a kid twelve years old in college—that makes it tough!"

"What are you trying to get across?" I asked.

Peck scratched his head. "I've spent a lot of time thinking about it. We all have. I guess we're here to sell America, to create understanding, to teach Indian students about the United States, and then go back and interpret India to the homefolks. The Indians usually have a very bad picture of America, so I guess we accomplish most just by showing them what Americans really look like."

Jerry Lewis sat up in bed. He had saved a tangerine from dinner and began to peel it while he talked. "For a long time I've been wondering what good we can do here. Gram Guenther always said we'd be amazed at how much was possible just by being ourselves. We've stumbled around, but I guess it's true. Our college principal told me that our informality, our songs and yells, was so unlike the British that it changed the students' whole attitude toward the West."

"I'd *like* them to understand America!" Ed said, raising his voice. "I can tell them about America. My father used to sell vegetables from a cart in New York. That isn't easy for them to believe in India. They think people who sell vegetables will always sell them. This is where the Communists come in with their appeal. I felt we did a lot of good against the Communists in those back country colleges where there's a strong leftist element —even if they weren't making themselves obvious."

"There's a limit to how much we can do though," Jerry interrupted. "When a businessman like Haley Mathews has no idea of the kind of life his working people lead, it shows you what you're up against."

"Well, I'd like to see Project India expanded," Ed continued. "I'd like to be on a Project Russia team. I'm sure we could help. I think people would learn something if we could exchange with the Russians, even if we sent a fumble-fingered group like ours." With that, Ed returned to his letter-writing.

Jerry Lewis neatly folded a tissue around the tangerine peelings and dropped the wad into a wastebasket. Then he said:

"I really believe I've learned to appreciate the Indian point of view. They seem to be in the position we were in fifty or a hundred years ago. That is, they want to be neutral and take time to build themselves up. They've got boys like Allen, our guide from the Law College. He's the kind that will do something about the caste system, and perhaps we helped him by making friends with him. It's hard to tell.

"One thing I know. I think I've changed my plans. I'd like to do a job like Chester Bowles did as ambassador to India. Any Indian will tell you he did a great job. He was one with them."

I said good night to Ed and Jerry. I left their room, which was in an outside wing of the T.B., and walked to the front door in the rain. At that hour of the night, the central hall of the T.B. was like the railroad station scene in *Gone With the Wind*. The bodies of sleeping men were strewn all over the cement floor. It was hard, but it was dry, and they had come in off the street when the downpour started. They were a melancholy sight from another world. I wondered whether Jerry Lewis, for all his honest good will, or any American, would ever become one with them.

NEXT morning, we were up early. The central hall of the T.B. was empty and Paul, the manager, seemed to have no idea that fifty or so non-paying guests had slept there the night before. He fed us a good breakfast, and by 8:30 we were off on a forty-three-mile drive to the town of Alleppey.

About half-way, we came to a lake which crossed the path of our highway. A ferry boat carried us to the other side. On board there was a ragged young man whose legs were three times the normal size. He suffered from elephantiasis, for which Alleppey was the plague-spot of south India. Harold Otwell was riding with us and explained that one out of five people in the town had the disease. The California students could see signs of elephantiasis all along the roadway: young and old alike had feet, ankles, and legs grotesquely and permanently swollen, painful to walk on, terrible to see, and ultimately fatal.

Our first stop was the factory of Peirce, Leslie & Co., Ltd. where the manufacturing of rugs and door mats, woven from coir fibers, had been put on a semi-mass production basis. The visit was arranged for Project India by the local Rotary Club, which was to be our host for lunch before the visit to Sanatana Dharma College.

A Mr. Verghese, the manager and a Rotarian, guided us around his plant. Coir, he explained, is a fruit something like the coconut. Coir meat, when dried, makes an excellent fibre. He led us into one hot, dusty factory room after another, each with empty fire-buckets on the walls. His workman furiously sewed up the edges of door mats, painted stencils on long hall runners, mixed dyes in steaming vats, or simply untangled endlessly tangled mounds of fibre. Unlike Panbkad, the coir factory was *all* noise, but it had the same sadness about it.

Weaving at top speed for his full eight hour day, a worker averaged one-and-a-half rupees (thirty cents) a day during the season, plus a year-end bonus of one hundred rupees. The factory employed four hundred men who could turn out 22,000 square feet of all kinds of matting in a day, representing a rough minimum gross of 22,000 rupees ($4,400). The cost of labor, then, was four per cent of the gross, a figure that probably had old Samuel Gompers whirling in his grave. Mr. Verghese quoted his figures with a certain pride, but Rosemary and Ruth, behind whom he walked most of the time, offered him no compliments. Everett and Jerry both were ashen-faced throughout the tour, and the rest of us sulked along without comment. I think Mr. Verghese was happy to get us out of there.

After the Rotary Club lunch, at which even Lerner and I were asked to say a few words, we went to Sanatana Dharma College. It was a colorful place with a small student jazz band parked under a palm tree playing American music, two hundred girls in brilliant saris, and a sprinkling of naked children, cavorting in the sandy soil.

When the team finished singing, "Vio, Vio, Viola," the rains came, but the principal insisted on carrying out *his* side of the program. This included a close order drill demonstration by student members of the National Cadet Corps, India's version of R.O.T.C. and C.C.C. combined. The boys snapped to attention in pouring rain. They were led through a series of marches until their heavy wool uniforms were soaked through. When they were thoroughly bedraggled, the principal called off the demonstration, and we made ready to leave.

A delegation from the National Student Federation had invited Project India to visit the Federation headquarters on the way home. The Federation was the all-India front organization for Communist activity among college students. It was a noisy group, but by no means did it represent a majority of the students at Sanatana Dharma College.

Project India was always willing to debate with Communist students, but had found them few and far between this year in south India. Eagerly, they accepted the invitation, only to find that Federation headquarters was in a tiny store across from the main college building. Jaffie decided that making a visit in plain view of non-Communist students who were still waving farewell to us would increase unnecessarily the Federation's prestige. But having accepted, Jaffie felt we must at least stop.

When the jeep pulled up in front of the Federation headquarters, a dozen boys charged out, shaking their fists and shouting Communist slogans in Malayalam. They threw open the jeep door, and I thought they were going to drag Thomas, the driver, right out of his seat. Instead, they abruptly pulled out their autograph books and begged for signatures! The Americans scribbled their names, the Federation boys cheered, and we drove off leaving them laughing in the rain.

Such was our first scrape with the Reds.

11 THAT EVENING, OUR LAST ON THE MALABAR COAST, WE MOVED INTO THE SPLENDID MALABAR HOTEL ON WELLINGDON ISLAND. JUST AS THE LIGHTS WERE FLASHING ON OVER in Ernakulam and across the bay in Cochin, we arrived there from Alleppey. The hotel was the sort of place Somerset Maugham has described often enough—uniformed bearers, a billiard room, an intimate bar, and an assortment of extremely British tea planters and businessmen sprinkled about the sitting room. The S.S. *President Polk* was anchored now in the harbor and its purser, a former U.C.L.A. student named Dick Banks, had brought some elderly American tourists in for the evening. Americans! We were delighted to see them.

Before dinner we bathed in deep tubs, and afterward we slept under mosquito nets in soft beds. Next morning our eggs were served surrounded by potatoes and sausages. We relaxed. By mid-afternoon we would be on the train for Madras and points north, discomfited again, but it was not an unpleasant prospect. Meanwhile, we were free to abandon ourselves to tourism.

M. C. Allen, the Law College student, came by early in the morning to escort the members of Project India on a sight-seeing tour of Fort Cochin and Mattancheri, the twin cities of Cochin Island. The girls decided to spend the morning repairing their clothes and their femininity, so again the group was made up of Allen, Jerry Lewis, Ed Peck, Everett Brandon, and Joe Michels.

For a penny apiece, a hungry-looking oarsman rowed the group acorss the half-mile stretch of open water to the Mattancheri embarcadero. Once on land, the boys climbed a steep stairway to the entrance of a maharajah's palace. Next door was a garden in which there was a Hindu temple with a domed roof and a sacred cow who enjoyed a limitless supply of good green grass. Beyond the farthest garden wall was the clock tower of the Pardesi Synagogue at the upper end of Synagogue Lane in Jewtown, a ghetto in Mattancheri.

Inside the maharajah's palace, which was now a museum, the California students went from room to room, bending down to avoid hitting their heads on low doorways and ogling ancient murals. Most of the murals depicted a god's earthy prowess with a dozen or more pretty young goddesses—simultaneously. The gamey nature of Hindu religious art came as a surprise to them, but they managed to keep studious looks and straight faces.

Allen led them out into the sunlight again and around the garden wall to Bazaar Street, the main thoroughfare of Cochin Island. In a few minutes they crossed the line into Jewtown and entered Synagogue Lane. It would not be remarkable to see such a street in Portugal, but here it seemed to be make-believe.

Looking north from where they stood, one could see the Pardesi Synagogue on the west side of the street, flush against the maharajah's garden wall. The lane was a cul-de-sac. Two rows of identical two-storied houses led up to the wall, and one hardly noted their shuttered windows and orange-tile eaves. Rather, the lane was like a miniature canyon, smooth on two sides and sealed at the end. Here lived the eighty remaining "white" Jews of Cochin, and because it was Saturday the lane was absolutely empty.

At the synagogue two men came forward to greet the Americans. One was a small old man with a stubby white beard. He was Saul Koder, the sexton. He wore a candy-striped skull-cap, a multicolored vest, and flowing striped bloomers. He spoke Malayalam and a little English. With him was a thin young man in white duck shorts named Jack Cohen, who helped Mr. Koder whenever his English failed him. Together, they exhibited the synagogue.

Most of the white Jews' ancestors, Jack Cohen said, had come to Cochin during the Inquisition; they had been driven from Europe and from Goa, a Portuguese enclave on India's west coast. They built the Pardesi Synagogue in the year 1568 on the site next to the garden wall, because the land had been given to them, tax-free forever, by a kindly maharajah.

The synagogue had one large room with three windows on each side and no place to sit. The *tebah,* a brass-railed altar from which the Torah was read, was in the center of the room, and the arc was at the far end, placed so the people could face west to Jerusalem when they prayed. Several bunches of brass oil lamps hung from the ceiling. The floor was covered with blue and white Chinese tiles.

Mr. Koder told us that the tiles first belonged to a maharajah

who had received them as a gift from a Chinese merchant. When
the maharajah had learned that the tiles were painted with cows'
blood, he was unable to use them in his palace and so gave them
to his neighbors who had no scruples about cows.

At the arc, Mr. Koder parted the curtains to show us the old
Torahs. He opened one to show the Hebrew script.

"We've got people who can read it," Jack Cohen said, "but who
can understand what it means? There hasn't been a rabbi here in
decades."

Joe Michels wandered about the room, staring up at the
women's gallery in the rear balcony, watching the Eternal Light
above the arc, and breathing in the strange tradition that hung
like a fog in the room. Young Joe sought experience for its own
sake, and he was enjoying himself immensely.

When the California students left the synagogue, Jack Cohen
made himself a member of the group, serving as co-guide with
M. C. Allen.

"Jews are very strange," Allen said, quietly shaking his head.

Cohen's first act was to point out the clock tower above the
synagogue. There were clock faces on three sides of it, each with
different numerals: one Hebrew, one Malayalam, one Roman.

"That way everyone knows what time it is," he explained. "And
many people don't have clocks of their own. Our people here are
quite poor, except for one man, also named Koder. He lives way
up the other end of the island in a big house."

Cohen waved his hands in the air as he walked and talked. There
was an American pitch to his voice, and he had mastered the
American idiom.

"I've lots of friends in America," he said. "Some boys from New
York were here during the last war. This was a tough little island
in those days. The police had to crack a few skulls and that sort
of thing—right here on Bazaar Street."

Now and then Cohen waved to someone.

"That's my cousin," he'd say, or, "There's my uncle," until it
was plain that he was related to every "white" Jew on Cochin. He
had nothing to say about the "black" Jews of Cochin who had lived

along the Malabar Coast for 1800 years. Most of them had now gone to Israel.

"Some of *us* have gone to America in recent years," Jack went on, "but visas are hard to come by. Israel is the place for us. Business here is lousy. In 1948, the Indian government started taxing land that we'd held for hundreds of years tax free. It's made the difference between keeping our heads above water and going broke. The people are moving now. Israel, it's a magnet. We'll all be gone sooner or later."

Having long since left Jewtown, Allen and Cohen led the way across the line that separated Mattancheri from Fort Cochin on Bazaar Street. In a warehouse section, the name of an old British shipping firm was being repainted on the door of a storage bin. It was an august name from the days of the Empire.

"The British. They still take all the money out of India," Cohen said. "I make no bones about it. This is my home. I'm an Indian nationalist."

Abruptly then, he pointed his finger at a huge house painted a dull autumn red.

"That's *the* Mr. Koder's house," he said, respectfully.

On the first floor, Mr. Koder had one of many provision stores he owned up and down the Malabar Coast. His home was on the second floor behind the gingerbread and gables that some Dickensian colonial officer must have had designed for himself years ago.

I was the only one who wanted to meet Mr. Koder, so while Everett, Ed, Joe, Jerry, and Allen went on to watch fishermen working their ancient Chinese nets, I ran up the backstairs of the Koder house with Jack Cohen. A servant ushered us into Koder's formidable living room. It was filled with ornate furniture, mahogany screens, and thick draperies. The place needed a good soaking in daylight.

Mrs. Koder, a huge woman, lumbered into the room wearing a black dress that just did hold her in. Like the room, she was neither Indian nor Portuguese, ancient nor modern. She was distressed when I told her I'd been in Ernakulam a week and had not come by earlier to meet her husband. Now he had gone away for the week-end. She was even more distressed when I said I could not stay for lunch. Finally, she urged me to visit her mother who lived at the Grand Hotel in Calcutta. After about five minutes of this, I made my excuses, grabbed Jack Cohen, and fled.

Allen and the four Californians were waiting outside. Bob Jaffie and Harold Otwell had arrived in the jeep via the island's mainland bridge and offered to drive them back to the hotel. Lerner and I climbed in, but the boys had another plan.

They chartered a tiny skiff, whose mainsheet looked like an early American quilt, and sailed across the bay to the hotel!

JAFFIE's Project India team was scheduled to begin another round of college visits two days hence in Guntur, a town on the east coast of India in Andhra state. It meant a five-hundred-mile train ride for them. Lerner and I were to leave them at the halfway station—Madras—and fly north to join Gram Guenther's team in Calcutta. So after lunch, Thomas drove us to the railroad station, where we said goodbye to him and to Harold Otwell, who had been a good companion for the past week.

Our compartment had four lower berths and four uppers, each parallel to the tracks for easier sleeping. During the day, the compartment may seat sixteen travellers, eight of whom have to get out at night and sleep somewhere else. By train time, however, no extra passengers had come along, and we had the compartment to ourselves for the overnight ride to Madras.

The lowers were comfortable hair mattresses, upholstered with green leather; but the uppers, which pulled down from the wall, were mere green leather stretchers only slightly more comfortable than the beds we had slept in in the Traveller's Bungalows. Rosemary and Ruth would double up on a lower berth so there would be sleeping room for the nine of us.

For our evening meal we had box lunches prepared and packed for us at the Malabar Hotel. It was like a picnic. Afterward, when the train pulled into a small town called Coimbatore, Ed Peck unlocked the door and ordered tea from a tea-butcher on the station platform. The man ran off, the tails of his turban flying in the air, to get the water boiling. About ten minutes later the train began to roll. We heard the shouts of the tea-butcher above the sounds of steel wheels grinding on steel rails and the shrieking of the train whistle. Ed Peck threw open the door again.

Four men, with the tea-butcher in the lead, were running down the platform toward our compartment. The leader carried a tray with two hot water pitchers; the second man ran with an armload of cups; the third man had a stack of saucers; and the last man had a milk pitcher and a sugar bowl! At the last possible moment, the tea-butcher flung himself into our compartment with his hot water pitchers sliding dangerously on the tray. The three bearers, who by this time were having trouble running on the cinders in the railyard, passed over the cups, saucers, and condiments. Each man was gasping for breath and, as he completed his mission, fell by the wayside, spent.

We, of course, now had not only the tea, but the tea-butcher as well, locked in our compartment while the train gathered speed and rumbled into the night.

He was the only inscrutable man I ever saw in the Inscrutable East. He neither spoke nor smiled. Squatting Indian-style on his haunches with his bare feet flat on the floor, he poured tea for us. He did not offer milk or sugar, although most Indians drink tea with both. The tail of his turban had fallen over one eye, but he did not bother to brush it away.

We felt sorry for him at first. Poor fellow, carried off into nowhere for 18-annas worth of tea, he deserved our pity. Upon mature reflection, however, we began to pity ourselves. If there were no more station stops until morning, how could we sleep with this stranger in our compartment? Many Indians had told us tales of banditry and murder on the railroads with all the relish of tabloid crime reporters. Perhaps this man selling tea was part of a plot! Another look at the inscrutable figure hunched over his steaming teapots convinced us that *trouble* was brewing.

Fifteen minutes later, the train arrived at another station. The tea-butcher quietly collected his cups and saucers and disappeared in the throng on the platform. He probably caught the next train west for home. We were not sorry to see him go.

Joe Michels, Jerry Lewis, and I were sitting on a lower berth. At different times, each of us had gone into the water closet to change into our pajamas. Now the talk drifted to religion. Jerry Lewis said:

"In San Bernardino, I'm not closely connected with any church. I used to go to a Baptist church, but it was more social than anything else. I felt like a hypocrite going for social reasons, so I stopped going. But I've been reading philosophy lately, and I have a terrific interest in religion. I'd like to find something."

Joe Michels borrowed a cigarette from me and said, "Ever since I started reading Indian philosophy, I dreamed of going to India. I knew it would be a great experience in my life, a turning point. I know I'm only eighteen and younger than anyone else here, but I'm sure this trip will influence my whole field of study.

"At one time I was a Christian Scientist. Now I'm a pantheist. I read about it and found it to be the oldest of all religions. I felt that if I was to retain a belief in God, it had to be something like this, without dogmas. This is my transition stage. Pantheism is an excellent belief to have while studying other religions."

Joe's background was probably Protestant, but he never discussed his parents, who were divorced. But through his own search for a religion, or, at least, a safe idea, he was able to look at the world in a way that was different from the other students'. It gave him a special perspective on their common experience of India:

"When I see the poverty here and refer it back to Indian culture, I can see where the Hindu idea of resignation comes from. And also reincarnation. Without *that*, there would be nothing at all.

"One thing that has interested me a great deal is the motive behind the questions we've been asked. Communist propaganda is behind many questions, like 'Is Dulles a warmonger?' and 'Why do Americans fear Communism?' but I think the lack of knowledge that lies behind such questions is more important than the question itself.

"I think our team can do good here. We show them the similarities between our exuberance and theirs, between our beliefs and theirs. Now I don't think you can feed people friendship on a spoon. When you feel close to each other, when you begin to understand each other's culture, that's how you make friends.

"I'm not outraged anymore by what I see here. The shock came to me immediately after I got off the plane in Bombay. I was horrified. I wanted to go home. But then I tried to understand how it came to be. I didn't want to be outraged, nor did I want to be a hypocrite and say everything I saw was great. I don't blame the people for what isn't their fault. I was most impressed by what an Indian professor said to me—that there was no concept of freedom, only resignation, in India before the British came. Then it took people like Gandhi and Nehru, he said, to tell the people about freedom. This idea of free choice that we have is just now becoming known to many Indians.

"I really love these people. A lot of things I see, like the cheering crowds and the crowding around, are childish. But the expressions on their faces, the friendliness when they see you, that's what I admire. Affection seems to pour out of them. I don't like it when Indian students want to hold my hand, but in many respects it is wonderful that they are affectionate among themselves.

"Very few Indians have impressed me as individuals, but I could say that about Americans, too. When they are together they laugh a lot, and when they are alone with you they are self-conscious. *You* have to break the ice."

Joe talked a while longer, our train rattled on, Rosemary and Ruth were already asleep with their heads at opposite ends of their lower berth, Jaffie was writing a letter to his wife, and the rest of the team was moving in and out of the water closet preparing for bed. There was general agreement that the taller men should sleep in the upper berths, which were slightly longer than the lowers. I climbed into mine after Joe turned in, rolled up in my sheet, and went to sleep in seconds.

Next morning we breakfasted on tangerines, cookies, and water and arrived in Madras just before lunch. Lerner and I said "*Namesthe*" to the team, got off the train, and rode a taxi to the Madras airport. Late that same afternoon, we touched down at Calcutta's Dum Dum airport, a hectic place which suited the city it served. Here the people were different, the language was different, and the pace of life was different. And, of course, Gram Guenther and the other six members of Project India were different, too.

PART 3   *Deep in the Heart of Bengal*

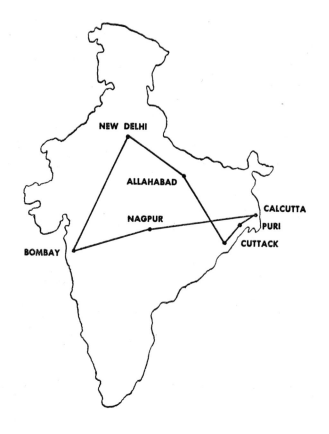

ROUTE OF THE NORTHERN TEAM

12 ON A DOUGLAS DC-4, OWNED BY INDIA'S NATIONAL AIR-
LINE AND FLOWN BY TWO SIKHS WITH HEROIC BLACK
BEARDS, OUR FLIGHT FROM MADRAS TO CALCUTTA WAS
smooth and uneventful, except that we landed at one place where
there was no air control tower, nor even a sock to show which
way the wind was blowing.

Lerner and I were met at Dum Dum Airport by an official with
a message from Gram Guenther. The substance of the message was
that it was cheaper for Lerner and me to take the bus to Calcutta
than it was for the seven of them to meet us at the airport. Gram
was very economical, especially when it came to transportation.
We, of course, had half-expected to be met, but now we realized
that rapport was not transferrable; we would have to start from
scratch again, building a new relationship between the members
of the Calcutta team and ourselves. So we took the bus.

At the terminal in Calcutta, the moment we stepped down to
the sidewalk, seven pairs of eager American hands seized us. Out
of nowhere, wreaths of bright red flowers were flung about our
necks. Our bags were snatched from our hands, and at any moment I expected to be hoisted in the air on somebody's shoulder!

Gram, Sandy Ragins, Patti Price, Ron Pengilly, Mary Ann
Buford, Bob Stein, and George Wakiji were all talking at once.
They wanted to know how we were feeling, how the southern team
was feeling, how we thought *they* were feeling, was it true about
the cheering students who had greeted us in Travancore, didn't
we have any trouble at all, was the food good, and so on and so
on, until Lerner and I lost all hope of answering their questions
coherently. Instead, we started asking them questions, and this is
what we learned.

They had worked very hard in Calcutta after that first placid
week in Nagpur on the way across India from Bombay. At Howrah
Station, Calcutta's huge railroad depot on the Hooghly River,
they had been met by a modest crowd of Indian students who
had known members of Project India in past years. It was good
to know that the Indians' friendship had endured. They had
crossed the great Howrah Bridge into the heart of the city, and
it was a different world from any they had ever seen. The streets

were alive with coolies, Sikhs, bike-riding clerks, refugees, cows, goats, rats, vendors, fakirs, policemen, peasants, beggars, sweepers, bullocks, horses, sheep, crows, vultures, monkeys, tourists, Parsis, Tibetans, Nepalese, Westerners, Chinese and small children—all swirling in, about, and around a tangle of rickshaws, taxis, trolley cars, autos, and double-deck buses. They had never seen anything like it. Nothing they had imagined could equal it.

Calcutta had thriving industries, a stock market, good hotels, and Western-style night clubs. It had a race track, tons of monuments to British rulers and British heroes which no one looked at, and hundreds of unreconstructed Englishmen whom everyone tolerated. And it had untold numbers of Communist agitators who devoted their time to the economically and psychologically depressed classes of the city—to the refugees from East Pakistan, the unskilled laborers, the underpaid white collar workers, and the chronically unemployed paupers who ate, slept, lived, and died on the curbstones of every street.

Everywhere, Calcutta was seething—intellectually, emotionally, and religiously. From the beautiful Jain Temples in Buddree Das Temple Street to the blood-stained Kali Temple in the Kalighat section, its soul was Hinduism; tents, tenements, modern apartments, and five-story office-buildings were its body; and the University of Calcutta, to which were allied twenty or more colleges, was at least part of its mind. Project India went straight to the University.

They began nervously, but by the time Lerner and I landed they were frequenting every center of student life in Calcutta —including the India Coffee House on College Street in the center of the University area, students' hostels, canteens, book stores, common (recreation) rooms, and tea houses. They were making the formal type of presentation which had been the stock-in-trade of Jaffie's team. And they even stood on street corners talking to collegiate-looking passers-by.

Usually they had to make their own contacts at a college. Most of the time they wrote letters by way of introduction, but once in a while they walked in cold and started talking, either to the college principal or to a group of students. Once they got a foot in the door, they arranged further meetings, discussion groups, and school assemblies. It was an exasperating, nerve-wracking business.

The United States Information Service, headed up during this summer by Thomas Needham, Public Affairs Officer, had a general policy of non-identification with Project India, in contrast to the U.S.I.S. policy in south India as expressed by Harold Otwell. As individual Americans, Calcutta members of the U.S.I.S. were hospitable to the group; but Needham wanted to make the truth quite obvious.

Project India, he said, was not part of, or speaking for, or secretly in cahoots with, the State Department; his chief concern was that the Californians in India should be well-informed and, at the end of the summer, should leave behind more Indian students favorably disposed toward Americans than when they came.

The U.S.I.S. policies had some justification, I thought. In south India, the student bodies and, indeed, the faculties of the colleges, were less sophisticated, less sanguine, and relatively far from the center of India's political storms. They were unlikely to resent an apparent, even though unofficial, association with the United States Government in the person of Harold Otwell, the U.S.I.S. Librarian.

Calcutta, on the other hand, was very close to the dead center of Indian political activity. It had known dreadful days, famine, riots, strikes, unemployment, and bloodshed. If any city in India was a powder-keg, it was this capital of West Bengal state, the Texas of India. The Bengalis were a volcanic, aggressive, hard-headed race, compared to the people of Malabar, who were themselves far more volatile than the Americans. A Bengali might have interpreted a phone call from U.S.I.S. as a sure sign that Project India was a suspicious State Department operation. Needham would not take this risk, so the Calcutta team was on its own.

In spite of the great enthusiasm they had shown for Lerner and me, the Calcutta team was a tired-looking band of patriots. They had been up every morning for the past week at 5:30 to be on their "work project" by 7:00 A.M. George Wakiji had a severe

case of diarrhea. Gram had been ill. Mary Ann Buford, the tall
Negro girl, had been plagued for three days by an uncompleted
cable-telephone call from Los Angeles. She did not know whether
it was her father calling with bad news or whether it was only
her friend Dennis, a young man who'd given her some luggage
as a going-away present.

All the rest, Patti, Sandy, Ron, and Bob, had been bed-ridden
at least once in the past three weeks in Calcutta. The heat, the
humidity, the food, and fatigue were a kind of conspiracy against
them.

One thing, however, made life easier for them than it had
been for previous Project India teams in Calcutta. The Geneva
Conference, which produced the now-famous Geneva Spirit, had
hardly been mentioned in south India, but next to the march on
Goa on Independence Day (August 15th), it was the big news
event of the summer in Calcutta. The papers were filled with
headlines and stories saying that the cold war had ended. President Eisenhower's role at the conference was described in the
most glowing terms. None said that what really happened was
a change of Russian tactics, but for the summer at least, the word
"warmonger" was omitted from the lexicon of anti-American
students.

Yet in spite of the improved political climate, the basic problem
remained: how to make friends with Calcutta students, using an
approach that was quite different from that of the team in south
India.

Sandy Ragins, the student-leader of the group, was a fair-
haired, blue-eyed Jewish boy with the highest average grades
of all twelve U.C.L.A. students. He was the son of a Los Angeles
lunchstand proprietor, who had been killed in an auto accident
in 1954. His mother worked as a saleswoman in a Jewish bakery.
Sandy was nineteen years old, a member of the class of 1956,
majoring in something called Special Studies, which included
roughly equal portions of sociology, philosophy, and English
literature. In his spare time, Sandy studied Hebrew and was already accepted at the Hebrew Union College, a rabbinical school
for Reform Jews in Cincinnati.

When I had met Sandy in Washington, he had been very much concerned about my journalistic integrity and the "slant" of the magazine for which we worked. He was quite within his rights, but it had irritated me. In Calcutta, however, he seemed as happy to see Lerner and me as the rest.

Patti Price was sort of a brunette Betty Hutton. She had thick eyebrows, brown hair, a tilted nose, and a vivacious smile. She was the prettiest girl of the four in Project India, but she was not at all concerned with the boys on either team. Even though she had told me that her only ambition in life was marriage, she was too busy growing, talking, and absorbing at break-neck speed to be much concerned about it. She was twenty years old, the daughter of a Standard Oil of California personnel man in Taft, California, an Episcopalian, a firm Republican, and a sorority girl. Her major subject was English literature.

Patti's husky voice and boundless energy were dominant factors within the group in Calcutta. They were the spur, the trusty support, the cause of a headache now and again, but largely indispensible to the team.

Ron Pengilly was an athletic, red-haired Presbyterian boy, twenty-one years old, with more freckles than Bob Jaffie. His home was in Montebello, California, near Whittier. His father was dead, and his mother somehow managed two full-time jobs for herself, one as a night nurse, the other as a daytime real estate insurance saleswoman. Ron himself was no stranger to work, having held early morning and late afternoon jobs since his high school days. He was as deeply conservative as Sandy Ragins was liberal.

At U.C.L.A. he belonged to a fraternity and aspired to Harvard Law School. He was majoring in political science and economics. Ron had received a scholarship from U.C.L.A. for each of his three years and, on the basis of his B-plus average, it was to be extended for his final undergraduate year.

Ron and Sandy, Gram told me, had both left their positions on either side of the political center and had moved closer to one another while in Calcutta. They had argued bitterly and had disagreed violently, but their common experience tended to change both of them. In a country that was both socialist and underdeveloped, Sandy began to acquire a deeper concern for the preservation of individual initiative, while Ron began to show a greater interest in the role of government in the field of social welfare. Both, I assume, will always vote for different political parties, but their clash and development was an unexpected dividend from Project India.

George Wakiji was a short, muscular young man, twenty-six years old, who had been a combat infantryman with the 45th Division in Korea. He roomed at a Japanese-American boarding house at school. His parents were Buddhists, but he subscribed to no particular religion. During World War II, like Ruth Taketaya, he was interned with his family at a camp in Arizona. Now his family lived frugally in Pasadena on his father's earnings as a nurseryman. George worked in the University library twenty-five hours each week and in a gas station, too, to pay his way through school.

He would graduate in June, 1956, with a major in social welfare. His marks were average, but he intended to get his Master's Degree and "work with kids." He was a Democrat, but had voted for Eisenhower.

Mary Ann Buford had broad shoulders, big hands, and dark brown skin. Her father was a fireman, and her mother worked on the assembly line at an electrical manufacturing company in Los Angeles. Although she was only twenty, she was president of the 62nd Assembly District Young Democrats and preferred her community activities to most campus affairs. She directed plays at her Methodist Church and played the organ. Her first year of college was spent in U.C.L.A.'s night school while she earned money in the daytime to pay for it. Now Mary Ann was a full-time day student with a scholarship; she majored in psychology and, after her senior year, wanted to go into clinical work. She was president of her sorority.

Bob Stein, twenty-one years old, was short and blond, with a crew-cut and baby-blue eyes. He was the son of a Beverly Hills movie distributor and theater owner. Stein was Jewish but not very religious. He was a "Big Man on Campus," and in the fall he would be president of Cal Club, which was President Robert Sproul's student advisory board from all the campuses of the University.

Stein said that he was a Democrat, but that he had only a passing interest in politics. He was majoring in psychology, making a C-plus average, and hoped to go into advertising or personnel work. First he would get his army service out of the way; he had been in R.O.T.C. throughout his university career and would be commissioned a second lieutenant.

Wakiji, Mary Ann, and Stein were a kind of unit in the Calcutta team, just as Sandy, Patti, and Pengilly were units in and of themselves. Soon after the team arrived in Calcutta, it was found that they could function effectively in twos and threes. Indeed, this was often found more desirable with small groups of Indians than the full six-member team. Sandy, Patti, and Pengilly were such strong personalities that one of them plus one or two of the group of Wakiji, Mary Ann, and Stein, were usually enough to hold a good-sized session in a canteen or at a college.

Personality is a subtle thing, however, and the less vibrant trio were as likely to spellbind an audience or make a friend as the three who somewhat overshadowed them. In south India, the personalities of the California students had been less important than the personality of the group as a whole, but things were different in Calcutta. Here, the California students very often talked to the same student two, three, or four days in a row at the India Coffee House, at their hotel, or in a hostel. Beyond the questions of international relations and U.S. domestic affairs, there were the simple questions of what kind of a person are you? do you like me? are we friends? how are we different? The appeal of personalities became as important as what individuals had to say. And, of course, the most vital personality of all was Gram Guenther, who was as sharp-eyed as when I had last seen her, but otherwise grayer, thinner, and even more intense than I would have imagined. She wanted her kids to succeed so badly!

WE had been jabbering away on the sidewalk in front of the Indian Airlines terminal, hardly aware that a crowd was gathering. After all, it was not every Sunday afternoon that Americans threw floral wreaths around the necks of other Americans in the middle of the sidewalk. When we finally got over the first rush of words, we were about to be surrounded. But the boys lifted our luggage and deposited it and us in a waiting taxi. The *taxiwallah*, like all hackies in Calcutta, was a bearded, turbaned, grizzly-looking Sikh.

"A taxi ride is very special for us," Sandy said.

"How so?" I asked.

"We never ride them during the week. It costs too much money, and even if it didn't the Indian students think it costs a lot of money and would feel we were being ostentatious. They ride the trams, so we ride the trams, too."

To my surprise, I noticed that Sandy's voice had a new accent. He had been trying so hard to make the Bengali students understand his English, that he had begun using their accent. Sandy sounded precisely like what he was: an American speaking English the way it was learned by a Bengali from the British. He had also picked up a few words of Hindi, which enabled him to tell the cab driver to go faster and to thank him for the ride when we reached the Russell Hotel.

The hotel was in Russell Street. You could get fed, barbered, shod, or entertained at a tiny sidewalk bazaar on the shady side of the street. The hotel itself was far back from the street, behind a stone wall in a well-tended yard. The building was plastered green outside and seemed to be crumbling from dampness. It really was a third-rate residential hotel, but to Lerner and me it seemed like the Plaza.

Our room was on the second floor overlooking the back yard and a row of cottages at the rear of the Russell Hotel property. Above and beyond we could see vultures sitting like shadows of death in the trees. The room was quite comfortable and came equipped with a hot water heater and a room boy, named Raham.

Raham's job required him to serve us as valet, maid, bellhop, porter, messenger, janitor, and watchman all day and all night. He was never far from our door and, indeed, often sat with his back against it for hours at a time. At night, he slept on the floor a few feet down the hall. Agreeable to a fault, fond of the Gunga Din salute, jolly, obsequious, and anxious to please, the sixty-year-old "boy" embarrassed us. You accepted his slavishness because it was the local custom, just as Americans living year-round in India accepted six domestic servants when they could not afford more than one in the States. Yet you felt ashamed.

Lerner and I were testing the springs of our beds when Ron Pengilly came to our door and invited us to Gram's room for tea. We followed him downstairs, out the back door, past the hotel kitchen, and across the back yard to the row of cottages I had seen from my window. Here lived the members of Project India, two boys in each of two cottages and Gram and the two girls in a third. Although covered by the same roof, each set of roommates had a private entrance, a sitting room, bedroom, and bathroom. The accommodations were cheaper than those in the main building and rightly so. They were damp, poorly ventilated, and uninsulated. The ceilings were low, and the back windows faced an alley. One night soon after the team arrived in Calcutta, a thief came in through the back window and stole Ron's wallet, which was never recovered.

These were melancholy rooms, and if it weren't for the bed springs and the hot water heaters, a set of rooms at Phillip's Traveller's Bungalow in Kottayam would have been a fair trade. Yet in spite of the monsoon, mildew, and mosquitos, the Calcutta team survived in the back yard of the Russell Hotel for five weeks —a record not to be considered lightly.

Tea with Gram in the morning before breakfast and late in the afternoon was a tradition by now. She liked to fuss with teapots, fruit, and pastry from Flurry's confectionary around the corner on Park Street, while her children gathered around her in the sitting room discussing the business of Project India. When we arrived, Sandy was going over the schedule for the rest of their stay in Calcutta, Gram was pouring tea, and Patti was condemning an item in a recent copy of *Time* magazine that she did not like. George Wakiji and Bob Stein were peeling plantains, and Mary Ann was carefully sipping her tea.

Relaxation is not an accurate word for what went on at tea

time. The Calcutta group worked with a greater sense of pressure, with more anxiety to succeed, than Jaffie's team. Sandy rattled off his list of things to come, the result of almost a month of planning, working, and hoping. Their work project—the building of a dispensary—was to be finished and dedicated; they were conducting a seminar, giving a party at the India Coffee House, and attending a final review session with the officers of Calcutta's United States Information Service; they were spending a weekend at a Community Development Project in a village near Calcutta; and they were making formal presentations at the University Law College, Bangabasi College, and St. Xavier's College.

It was a hectic schedule, calling for the last ounce of energy from each of them, beginning with tea at 5:30 in the morning and lasting all through the blistering, wet days until dinner at eight or nine in the evening. All seven of them accepted the pace as right and necessary. What drove Gram was not difficult to imagine: she had been to Calcutta three times before; she would not be satisfied by merely doing the same things over again. She was a restless soul for whom "seek and ye shall find" was a literal and categorical imperative. Her whole being was geared to a continual seeking; if sometimes it was a painful thing to watch, it was also an inspiration.

Sandy was a seeker, too, but the others—Patti, Ron, Mary Ann, George, and Bob—did not so easily reveal their motives.

I hoped I might understand all of them better as the days passed. Meanwhile, I would stand aside and watch. I never saw seven people work so hard in all my life.

13 AT FIVE O'CLOCK MONDAY MORNING THE CALCUTTA TEAM BEGAN ITS DAY. THE SUN WAS STRUGGLING TO MAKE DAYLIGHT, AND THE AIR WAS HEAVY WITH DAMPNESS. BY noon both the heat and the humidity would be over 90. Lerner and I joined Gram and the students in her parlor for breakfast. They were dressed in work clothes and muddy sneakers.

By six o'clock, we were ready to leave. Our destination was Santoshpur, a suburb of Calcutta, in which was located the site of Project India's annual work project. To protect themselves from the sun, the girls wore wide-brimmed straw hats, Ron Pengilly and George Wakiji wore pith helmets, and Sandy Ragins and Bob Stein wore caps. Stein's was a white cotton golfer's cap with the words "I am the Boss" printed across the crown.

The doors and shutters were locked, and we set off down Russell Street, passing the man with elephantiasis who always begged at the hotel gate. Soon we came to Chowringhee Road, the Fifth Avenue of Calcutta. On one side, the road was lined with apartment houses and commercial buildings—the famed Grand Hotel, a haven for Westerners and rich Indians from out of town, the smart shops and movie houses, and the offices of the United States Information Service.

On the other side, Chowringhee bordered Calcutta's village green—the Maidan—two square miles of grass, shrubs, and trees. The Maidan gave that jam-packed town a feeling of open space, without which Calcutta would have exploded more often than it did. On a big holiday, 500,000 people would flock there for an outing, milling around on their island of green in the drab city, watching the fakirs and pitchmen and acting like country people at an American country fair. Now the Maidan was quiet and almost empty. While we were walking through it, a company of soldiers practiced close order drill. The rhesus monkeys were sunning themselves in the tree tops, and a lazy goatherd let his goats wander where they pleased.

We reached our tram stop at last and caught a southbound car. Even at six in the morning, Calcutta's trams were stuffed with passengers.

We managed to thrust Gram and the two girls inside where six

109

seats were legally reserved for women. The rest of us hung on the outside as best we could.

We rode by the race track where grooms were walking a brace of sleek-looking horses, still steaming from their morning workout; we passed the Sikh troopers' barracks where the bearded warriors were busy with setting-up exercises. They were not wearing their turbans, but technically their heads were covered: they wore the delicate yellow ribbons in their hair which Sikhs may wear at home.

We rode through slums where large rats skittered across the street and a raven pecked at the eye of a dead goat and people made their toilets on the curb. Then abruptly Sandy gave the signal to disembark. We ran across the street and jumped on a low-ceilinged bus, once again hanging desperately to straps and posts.

The bus roared out of town and onto a narrow highway. When we had driven about ten miles from the Russell Hotel, I was beginning to wish the Californians had found a location closer to town for their good works. It was almost seven o'clock when the bus finally stopped and we stepped down. Only then did I realize that some of the younger Indians on the bus were University students come to lend a hand on the work project. About five of them got off with us and followed us along a dirt road through a rice field to the encampment known as Santoshpur.

Ever since the partitioning of India and Pakistan, Hindu refugees from East Pakistan had been streaming into West Bengal, just as Moslem refugees had been going the other way. Santoshpur was a tent village, like hundreds in the area, set up under the government's relief and rehabilitation program to house and care for the Hindu refugees. The people usually came into the state with nothing except the clothes on their backs and a few pots and pans. Now the little community (population 800) had an air of permanence about it, even though the people themselves were merely transients, hoping soon to move on to a new settlement where there was work.

During World War II Santoshpur had been the site of an antiaircraft battalion's encampment. Remnants of battlements and storage buildings were still standing. One of the latter had been converted into a school house. The village's one road, on which we were walking, was lined on both sides with the tents of refugee merchants in the grain, fish, or tobacco business. Mid-village, there was a well. Its two pumps were the main source of fresh water. However, back of the village, there was a reservoir in which people could bathe and catch an occasional fish. In recent months, the water level had dropped ominously. Even though it rained every morning between ten and noon and almost every afternoon about four, the monsoon this year was not as wet as usual. With all of their other woes, the people of Santoshpur also had a drought to worry about.

To the California students Santoshpur was the place where they could do something besides talk. They had wanted to put up a building in the Calcutta area as earlier Project India teams had done. Through a work project, they felt, they would contribute something concrete to India and at the same time demonstrate their belief that working with one's hands was (a) not beneath Americans and (b) a thing of dignity. In previous summers, through various U.S.I.S. and governmental contacts, Project India had arranged to build small school houses in nearby refugee villages. This summer it was suggested that this village, which already had a school house, badly needed a medical dispensary. So they got permission to build it.

The city of Calcutta provided bricks, mortar, a mason, and an engineer. Most of the sweat and muscle were provided by the Americans. They worked three hours every morning except Sunday, and the professionals, with help from a few local people, carried on until quitting time. At this rate they hoped to complete the job in about ten days. When I arrived, the walls were nearly up, the floor (twelve by fifteen feet) was about to be put down, and the roof was being assembled on the ground.

The area around the little red brick dispensary was littered with rusty buckets, stacks of bricks, and scatterings of straw, sand, and cement. Sandy Ragins and Ron Pengilly immediately stripped to the waist and set about mixing cement. George Wakiji peeled, too, sitting on a pile of bricks, which he commenced pulverizing with a hammer. The brick chips would be scattered over the dispensary floor at the proper time and covered with cement. The sun glistened in the big blue sky, and the day which had started out to be hot now became a sizzler.

Bob "I am the Boss" Stein was foreman of the job. He put Patti Price and Mary Ann Buford on water detail; they were to fill up a big drum standing in front of the brick pile. He organized some of the Calcutta University students into a sand-passing line. (When the work began a week before, few Indian students accepted the Americans' invitation to lend a hand; but now word of mouth in the India Coffee House had brought a score or more of willing workers.)

The work was not easy. Each brick had to be soaked in water before it was passed up to the mason. I never found out why, but I supposed that wet bricks held cement better than dry ones. The dispensary floor needed a mountain of pulverized brick, so they took turns breaking big chunks of brick into little pieces. They mixed cement within the crumbling walls of a nearby anti-aircraft site whose guns and camouflage had long since been moved away. The sand had been dumped back near the village road and since there were no shovels at Santoshpur, they scooped the sand into wicker baskets with a short-handled hoe and passed it down the line to a more convenient place. The Calcutta University boys were startled when Patti and Mary Ann got on the sand-passing line and shocked when Gram Guenther joined it as well. Later, after three lovely coeds in saris pitched in, they stopped working altogether just to watch them.

Everywhere excited refugee children were underfoot. To keep them amused and out of the way, Gram played nursemaid for a while each day. She gathered the children around her in one corner of the gun site and taught them to say "okay" and to whoop like *American* Indians. She asked them questions they did not understand, they answered with words she did not understand. She hugged them and petted them. Their laughter was like the ringing of very small bells. Gram and these small villagers played together until the children became restless; then Patti and Mary Ann came to relieve her.

By eight o'clock that morning, the girls' dresses were damp with sweat and flecked with sand. Their shoes and socks were wet and muddier than ever. Soggy, but unbowed, they led the refugee children to a clearing far from the work area and taught them to play Drop the Hankie, London Bridge, and Ring Around the Rosie. There were fifty or sixty of them in the ring around Rosie. Mothers, too, came to watch. They wore plain white saris and most of them carried very young babes on their hips. They did not smile easily, but they seemed to approve what was going on.

Skipping, running, and clapping their hands until I thought one of them would drop from exhaustion, Patti and Mary Ann attempted to end the games after an hour. The children screamed for more, so they had to go on still longer.

Later, Patti told me that playing with the children was one of the most important experiences of her life. "It changed me," she said. "I've always been afraid of kids, and then Gram said take the kids. I found them so unspoiled, so unprejudiced. They gave me their confidence and love. And then I wasn't afraid."

Meanwhile, diligent George Wakiji hammered away on the brick pile. He sat astride two bricks, sweat pouring from under his pith helmet and down his chest, leaving clean streaks in the red dust that collected there. Periodically he had to interrupt his labors and go off in search of privacy; he still had dysentery.

Sandy and Ron, the arch political opponents, had become expert at mixing cement together—just the right amount of gray powder with the right amount of sand and water. The mason seemed well satisfied with their product. When finished with the cement, Ron took his place in the brick-passing line, and Sandy hauled water. Bob Stein, an efficient foreman, bustled about keeping people busy. He wore his "I am the Boss" cap at a jaunty angle. It amused the University of Calcutta students and helped smooth the way when Stein assigned one of them to a job that lacked glamor. Some of the Indian students worked devotedly, some worked once in a while, and a few loafed all of the time. But it seemed that the effort was giving most of them a new sense of accomplishment.

At a safe distance the villagers of Santoshpur watched the antics

of these strange youngsters from Calcutta and California. Each
morning, about the time we were arriving, the women swept
clean the dirt floors of their tents and washed the few utensils
they owned. Some went off in search of cow dung, which later
they flattened like flap-jacks and plastered on the walls of the
gun site to dry into fuel for their evening fires. Others washed
clothes or gossiped or looked after their babies, but always with
an eye on the dispensary. The men, unemployed and waiting for
rehabilitation, bathed, shaved, brushed their teeth with sticks of
wood, and relaxed for the day. It was a boring life for them, and
many of them naturally drifted over to watch the dispensary
going up.

At first the elders of the village had not welcomed the idea of
someone barging in uninvited to build a dispensary in Santoshpur.
They did not care that it had been recommended by Mrs. Renuka
Ray, India's Minister of Relief and Rehabilitation. The elders
had their pride and lots of it. Besides, they were skeptical. But
Mrs. Ray's influence prevailed. And gradually, as the Americans
arrived each morning with minimum of fanfare, a fondness grew
up between them and the sidewalk superintendents.

One day a gray-haired, gray-chested Indian social worker,
who had spent more than a year living among the refugees in
Santoshpur, explained the refugees' attitude:

"These people knew they needed help but they had to be
shown that they were not being used."

"Have they been shown?" I asked.

"All I can say is that every day more and more local people
are working on that building after your Americans go away. That
means they've decided that the dispensary is a good thing and
that it is being put up because it is a good thing and for that
reason alone."

Each morning at Santoshpur was the same. There was work to
be done and children to be distracted. Bob Stein found a new
solution for the latter: he organized a young people's brick-passing
line. The half-naked boys and girls fell into line with their shoulders touching. Patti and a Calcutta University student soaked the

bricks in water and handed them, one at a time, to the first boy. "Eeta! Eeta!" he chanted and handed the brick to the next child. Soon the air rang with their sing-song voices. They were calling out the Bengali word for brick.

At the end of the line, Sandy Ragins shouted "Bhalo! Bhalo! Good! Good!" in that fine Bengali brogue of his, and for a half hour or so the line functioned efficiently

In fact, everyone did such a good job that the dispensary was finished one day ahead of time. The dedication date, however, was not moved up correspondingly, because the Minister of Relief and Rehabilitation herself, Mrs. Renuka Ray, had been invited for the ribbon-cutting ceremony and her schedule was not likely to be flexible.

Thus, eleven days after work began at Santoshpur, we arrived an hour later than usual on a bus laden with Calcutta University students whom the members of Project India had invited to attend the dedication ceremonies. Most of them had worked at one time or another at the dispensary, but others were there to see for the first time what all the commotion was about. They represented half-a-dozen colleges within the University and some of their campuses were a long distance from College Street, but nevertheless they had all met the same bus and had arrived together—with us.

A huge canvas, like the tent of a desert chieftain, had been thrown up on the site of the dispensary. One side of the tent was lashed to the bamboo scaffold that still surrounded the dispensary. The other sides were held up by crooked poles. The tent had several deep bellies full of rain water dangerously straining its seams. Crowded together under the tent were about 150 refugee men and children; the women stood out in the sun, for Bengalis have no patience with the matriachy of Malabar!

Three girls from the University had brought flowered friendship bracelets (rakhis) for the male members of Project India. There was even an extra one for Bob Lerner, but none for me. I had met the girls—Miss Bhose, Miss Gose, and Miss Roy— earlier in the week when they were passing bricks and sand.

They had worn elegant saris that day, and I remembered asking one of them if she was worried about spoiling hers. Now I thought that perhaps my remark had been misunderstood.

But Miss Roy suddenly came up to me with a *rakhi* in her hand; she had made it from a flower taken from her own hair and a piece of string.

"We made a mistake in counting," she said cheerfully.

I told her it did not make any difference, but really it did, and I was glad to have my *rakhi*.

At one end of the tent, tables and chairs had been set up for Mrs. Ray's entourage and Bob Stein and Sandy Ragins, who would represent Project India. A cool breeze made us very comfortable under the tent although the sun had a particularly hot glare outside, where the crowd was growing larger by the minute. Everyone seemed to be talking at once, in English and in Bengali. The din had a holiday sound, full of laughter and excited voices.

Those who could not find room to stand under the tent sat on the pile of surplus bricks or formed admiring knots a few paces back from the dispensary and jabbered excitedly about the architectural wonder before them. When the children began to grow impatient, Sandy Ragins stepped out of character and led them in a series of those unfailing U.C.L.A. cheers.

Bob Stein meanwhile sat at the table calmly putting the finishing touches on a cardboard plaque, which was to be presented to Mrs. Ray. Each college of Calcutta University from which students had come to help build the dispensary was listed on the plaque, and modestly, down at the bottom, U.C.L.A. appeared as well. It was not a very impressive plaque, but then the dispensary was its own monument to the idea of working together.

Time passed slowly. Magnificent, lazy, white thunderheads boiled up around the edges of the sky. Some palm trees very far across the rice land began swaying as the breeze picked up. Mrs. Renuka Ray was not very late, but she *was* late enough, and I knew that Sandy and Gram and some of the others were faintly apprehensive. After all, the United States policy of sending arms to Pakistan had greatly complicated Mrs. Ray's problem with the refugees. It had increased the fears of many Pakistani Hindus,

Above: *Calcutta street scene: Ron Pengilly, Sandy Ragins, Bob Stein, Patti Price, and George Wakiji walk with university students along Chowringhee Road.*

Below: *At Santoshpur, the Calcutta team works on its dispensary with the help of refugee children and friendly students.*

*Ron Pengilly plays horse-and-rider
with a new young friend.*

In World War II battlement, George Wakiji chips brick for the dispensary floor.

Coeds from the University of Calcutta pass bricks to Sandy Ragins.

Mary Ann Buford and Patti Price play Drop the Hankie with refugee children.

*Gram Guenther has a proud moment
at the dedication of the dispensary.*

Above: *Mary Ann Buford leads her playmates in London Bridge.*

Right: *Bob Stein and Patti Price keep "Coffee House hours" in Calcutta.*

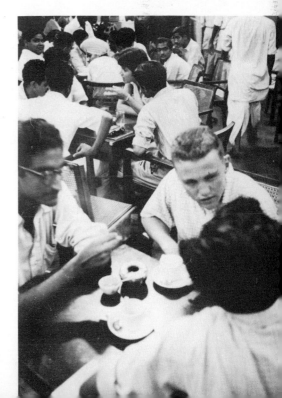

Above: *Sandy Ragins at Howrah Station gets a farewell gift of flowers from university students.*

Below: *Patti Price argues with a Sikh student on College Street corner.*

who logically concluded they might be safer across the border
in West Bengal. Increased fears led to increased immigration
which in turn led to increased headaches for the Indian ministry
of Relief and Rehabilitation. Mrs. Ray could be expected to assign
to the United States at least some of the blame for the resultant
misery.

To be sure, on the afternoon before the dedication, the Californians had heard Mrs. Ray praise them and their dispensary
building at a tea given by the governor of West Bengal state. But
something could have happened in the meanwhile to change her
mind.

Therefore, the shout which finally announced the arrival of
Mrs. Ray's party in a government car was one of the most welcome
noises of the summer. At first she could not get the door open
because the crowd swarmed around the car and pressed in tightly
on all sides. Then a path was made for her, and she walked slowly
to the tent, acknowledging with a faint smile the cheers of the
crowd. She was an abundant, handsome, graying woman wearing
a simply gray and blue sari. She was less delicate than, say,
Madame Pandit, but you could see that she was another one of
those brilliantly skillful Indian women of whom the world has
become increasingly aware since Indian independence. They
seem intellectual, motherly, and thoroughbred all at the same
time.

Following behind Mrs. Ray, her entourage consisted of several
gentlemen wearing semi-military uniforms—khaki shirts with
epaulets, khaki trousers, and heavy shoes, but no insignia—and
another man wearing a *dhoti*. Gram, Sandy, and Bob Stein greeted
them all respectfully and led Mrs. Ray to the doorway of the dispensary where she cut a red ribbon, looked in, and nodded thought-
fully. From there, Sandy led Mrs. Ray to the table at the front
of the tent. The crowd that had been so recklessly pushing and
shoving a moment before, now stood motionless waiting for her
to speak.

With magnificent aplomb Mrs. Ray began her speech—in Hindi!
She spoke for five minutes without uttering an English word. Once
or twice, the audience under the tent laughed at something she

said. The people outside, of course, could not hear, but they listened solemnly anyway. Obviously, all were pleased that she was talking the language of their country and had not, even for the sake of politeness, talked first in English. When she finished, there was wild applause for her and approving looks for the members of Project India. I have no way of knowing precisely what Mrs. Ray said in the Bengali dialect, but I assumed that it was fairly close to what she said in English:

"It is a thing of great wonder and great generosity for these young Americans to come far across the sea to visit India and to do more than talk about their affection, but actually to build something with their own hands that is needed and that will endure. This is the kind of contribution to understanding the world needs. . . ."

It was a flattering, unequivocal, happy speech. It dispelled all the earlier apprehensions about Mrs. Ray and made the work project seem not only successful but important, too.

Bob Stein kept his remarks brief and, with a restrained flourish, presented his cardboard plaque with the list of colleges on it to Mrs. Ray. On top of it, he placed an envelope containing 475 rupees for purchasing medical supplies. Mrs. Ray was touched and warmly thanked Bob Stein and the other California students. Gram, too, was moved; her eyes were misty and she wore a smile of joy, triumph, and relief.

Mrs. Ray walked back through the admiring throng, got in her car, and in a few moments was gone. It was time for all of us to go back to Calcutta. We went up the road, surrounded by village children, toward the bus stop. Three of the American boys were ahead of me. Sandy Ragins had an arm thrown around the shoulder of an Indian student as they walked. Ron Pengilly put his pith helmet on the head of a small boy and carried the boy on his shoulders. And George Wakiji walked slowly, head down, while small children held both his hands.

Just as the bus came, it started to rain. But the good deed was done, and no one much cared about the weather.

14 DURING THAT FIRST WEEK LERNER AND I WERE IN CALCUTTA, AFTER THREE HOURS OF HARD WORK ON THE DISPENSARY AT SANTOSHPUR, WE WOULD HAVE BEEN HAPPY TO SPEND the rest of the day in bed. But when the California students returned to the Russell Hotel around 10:30 each morning, bed was the farthest thing from their minds. Instead, they acted as though the three hours on the job were setting-up exercises. They showered and scattered to the various contact points which had been established with the University students: to college common rooms for a ready crowd of boys, to the India Coffee House off College Street for intimate conversations, to a student assembly for a formal presentation, or to street corners, canteens, and even private homes for a pot-luck selection of opportunities.

Their day rarely ended before nine in the evening. They worked singly, in pairs, and as a group. They would come back to the Russell Hotel for a bland luncheon, get more assignments from Sandy Ragins, and be off again. The pace was killing; so much was going on that Lerner and I had to decide whether to try to cover everything and spread ourselves very thin or to make a sampling of each *kind* of student contact and generalize. We decided on the latter course.

ONE morning, Sandy Ragins, Ron Pengilly, Bob Stein, Lerner, and I boarded the double deck bus at Park and Chowringhee and shuttled across town to a crowded street corner near Calcutta's Sealdah Railroad Station. The Station itself was clogged with refugees from East Pakistan who had set up house-keeping on the station platform. We walked up a side street, no wider than an alley, called Sealdah Market Street. It was a filthy street, tightly packed with open-air produce shops, cows, rickshaws, dogs, rats, and a raft of pitiful-looking peddlars. One hag in a tattered sari squatted in the midst of all this human and animal traffic fanning flies away from a tray full of silver fish which were spoiling in the sun. With a mechanical motion of her hand, she offered to sell us the fish; when we said no, she let fly a thin jet of betel juice, which splattered at our feet, and went back to her fanning. Another narrow street carried us away from the marketplace

119

and led to the gateway of Bangabasi College. It was a three-story building behind a brick wall, on which were plastered large sheets of newsprint. Fierce Communist slogans were painted on the sheets with bright red paint. These posters were the sole remains of a student election at Bangabasi College in which, by a narrow margin, the Communist-led Student Federation had lost its leadership of the student body.

We went through the gate and into the building, led by Sandy Ragins who always walked a little ahead of us. Round-shouldered and bent forward slightly at the waist, Sandy was like an eager bird dog, impatient with the scent and anxious to confront the bird itself face-to-face.

The Common Room of Bangabasi College looked like the recreation room of any small American college or the basement of a university fraternity house—except that it was more crowded. Over a hundred boys were in the Common Room playing bridge, dominoes, or Ping-pong, kibitzing the games, or merely sitting with friends for a chat between classes. The room was not small, but both light and ventilation were poor. After three boiling hours at Santoshpur, Sandy, Ron, and Bob Stein were about to subject themselves to a kind of human steam bath.

Immediately each of them was surrounded by a group of twenty or thirty boys, with more standing on chairs in the background. Lerner and I could neither get in next to them, nor hear from the outside what was being said. At the same time, we tried valiantly to keep similar groups from collecting around us. But it would have been easier to keep filings from attaching themselves to a powerful magnet; we were soon isolated from each other, each with his own group, and locked in debate over American race relations, the atomic bomb, and the situation in Goa.

The boys of Bangabasi pressed close to me, and every one smiled at every word I said.

In south India, I had shared the team's experience when I was trapped on the stage and pressed into singing "Vio Vio Viola" with them. Now, here was the Calcutta team's most basic experience, the kind of close-in relationship which was their stock-in-trade. In five weeks in Calcutta, they would be seen and heard

by 5,000 students—only one-sixth as many as the southern team
—but their relationships would have a depth unreached in the
south.

I would not have been very useful if I had been asked to carry
on this way for long. An hour at Bangabasi was all I could stand.
The Indian boys seemed nearly hysterical in their fondness for
Americans that morning. I began to sweat through every pore as
they pressed closer and closer around me. We talked of Geneva
and of Chester Bowles and Red China, and several times I had
to call time-out to wipe the steam from my glasses.

Somehow one boy got around to teaching me Hindi words—
I learned *nak* for nose, *dhanyava* for thank you, *ah-chah* for good,
teek-hai for okay, *chalega* for it will do, and something else, which
I've forgotten, for I love you, which I was to tell my wife when
I got home.

My attempts to learn a smattering of Hindi delighted the boys.
Their faces were all bright and shiny, the color of ginger-bread,
with black eyes and gleaming white teeth. They were noisy and
sweating and overwhelmingly good-natured; I felt that I was
drowning in a pool of good cheer. I badly needed a drink of water
and kept sucking my cheeks for saliva to wet my lips. My tongue
felt dry and sticky.

Then one boy shoved his autograph book under my nose, and
before I stopped writing I had signed my name dozens of times
on scraps of paper, the backs of envelopes, and sheets of notebook
paper. I had started out with my back to a wall, but now more
autograph collectors slipped in behind me and I was caught in
a huddle. I was a quarterback who did not know the signal for
"Dismiss!"

We went back to talking politics. Or rather I talked, and they
agreed with me, with anything I said. How I would have welcomed it if just one of them had shouted "Go home, American"
or anything that indicated there was one individual in this mob
of idolators! I felt an urge to smack one of those sweet smiling
faces which insulted me with adoration. I began looking for a
way out before I really did swing at someone or simply keeled
over from heat and nausea.

In the nick of time a boy plucked the back of my sleeve and said: "Would you like to go outside?"

I had not completely forgotten the Communist posters on the wall outside, so when I looked at the boy, I immediately found myself weighing the obvious immediate good that would result if I went with him against the possible subsequent evil that might befall me if the boy was bent on some positive demonstration of anti-Americanism. Then I took the hand offered to me and plowed through the crowd with my new friend leading the way. We burst into the fresh air, and it seemed to me that all of outdoor Calcutta was air-conditioned.

Four other students had been waiting for us. My new friend introduced me to them with all the pride of a hunter back from the jungle with his best kill by his side. For my part, I had no way of judging this quintet. My imagination was working overtime, no doubt, when I even sized them up physically—none of the five looked very tough.

But I think almost anyone would have been slightly suspicious. They were dressed alike—wearing white shirts, white-duck slacks, and brown shoes—and they whispered in everyone's ear but mine. When one of them took me by the arm and led me off down another alley, I could not help but get the idea that I was, indeed, caught in the toils of the Communist Party of India. Nevertheless, since all five of them seemed utterly harmless, I went along gaily, though not without a slight pang in my stomach. We crossed a main thoroughfare, went sideways between two buildings, and continued on in another alley. I was trying to remember the way, but already I was lost. And I was thirstier than ever.

"Can I get a cup of tea where we're going?" I asked.

The five boys laughed and shook their heads—yes.

By now my thirst was far stronger than my misgivings. I urged them to hurry. We walked rapidly for four or five minutes more, at last entering a street full of tobacco shops and hardware stores. At the end of the block, we went inside a red stone building with the words India Tea Room written over the door. The place was empty except for a group of boys at one table. They were listening to a harmonica player and drinking tea-with-milk out of water glasses.

A waiter came out of a back room, waved, and disappeared. When he returned, he carried on a tray six glasses of tea and a plate of sweetmeats. I drank deeply, burning my tongue, thankful for the blessed wetness, while my five escorts silently smiled upon me. Then they made me understand. One said:

"It was so crowded in the Common Room, we couldn't see any of you, so we decided on kidnapping."

"This is *our* common room," said another, proudly.

"They are always talking politics over at Bangabasi," said a third, with great disgust.

"To hell with politics," I said.

"So that is why we brought you here!" and they clapped their hands.

Then the harmonica player came over to our table and sat down with me and my non-political friends. We sang songs. Suddenly I decided that I liked these boys very much and vowed to stay away from mobs, lest I get an unfortunate opinion of Indian youth.

When I returned half an hour later to Bangabasi, Sandy Ragins was seriously considering the formation of a search party, and Bob Lerner was sadly convinced that the Reds had murdered me. The boys from the Common Room had not worried at all and when they walked us to the bus stop, I could see that they were highly amused by the reaction to my disappearance.

No doubt it was a fact that the Indians were not as afraid of Communists as we were; indeed, they were not afraid at all.

Bob Stein, who had not been bothered by the close quarters at Bangabasi, later on talked about communism among Indian students.

"From what I've seen, there are a lot of students here who think they are Communists until you define it for them," Stein said. "When we came to India, the world situation was different than it seems now since the Geneva Conference. Maybe it will change again. But right now the number of Indian students who even *say* they're Communists is very small, and when you define communism, many say they don't believe in it at all.

"It has a dramatic appeal to poor people and to students who are looking for a quick solution to India's problems. But from what I heard from previous Project India teams, I feel the Communist influence among the students has declined in the past three years. There have been some hard fights against the Communists in student elections at colleges like Bangabasi.

"In some places, even the 'good guys' have used tough tactics to win—stealing registration cards, threats, physical violence, things like that. Some of the student politicians don't associate means and ends at all.

"On the other hand, when it comes to America, I don't think we're dearly loved either. We're respected, sort of, and Eisenhower is quite popular since the Geneva business. But that is liable to be a disappointment. I mean, Geneva is just a step up the ladder, but none of the Indian students feel that conservatively about it."

Listening to Stein, I realized that if one could get accustomed to such pressure chambers as the Common Room at Bangabasi, there was indeed much to be learned.

WHILE Sandy, Ron, and Stein were visiting the Common Room at Bangabasi, the schedule called for Patti, Mary Ann, and George to go to the India Coffee House off College Street, the University's unofficial center for big bull sessions and small talk. Every day of every week, except Sunday, one or more members of the Calcutta team had "Coffee House hours"; that is, they spent two, three, or four hours at a stretch discussing the issues of the day with anyone who was willing to talk. It was not difficult to find talkative, inquisitive, or just friendly students at the Coffee House, and some of these, at least, were student leaders.

But it was not easy finding a *new* tableful of boys every day, and many hours had to be spent in the boring business of talking about the same issues with the same people. Again, what the Calcutta team had to do was hard work.

The India Coffee House was part of a chain of coffee houses than operating in most medium-sized or large cities in the country. It was half-a-block from the University of Calcutta campus in a heavily populated secondary business section. Its street was lined with bookstores, several of which prominently displayed such titles as *Three Essays by Lenin* and *The Constitution of the*

People's Republic of China in inexpensive paperbound editions. Comparable works from the United States were either unavailable or out of sight.

On the second floor of a gray stone building, after a steep climb up a flight of dingy stairs, the India Coffee House proved to be a surprise. While I did not expect candlelight, dark corners, and intimacy, neither did I expect a room the size of a basketball court. But the Coffee House was at least that big and twice as noisy. On the ceiling two dozen fans chopped through the air, fighting a losing battle against cigarette smoke and coffee odors. On the wall opposite the door coffee, tea, and cashew nuts were served up from a bar with a maximum of clattering efficiency. Scattered around the floor, there were about sixty coffee-tables and some two hundred chairs, all occupied and each a center of intellectual ferment, gossip, and laughter.

One day, Bob Lerner and I accompanied Patti Price to that upstairs den of conversation. The room was nearly full, and Patti had more or less her pick of the student groupings—she had been coming there so long that most of the Indian boys welcomed her and even vied for her company.

Looking over the crowd, I remembered something Sandy Ragins had said to me: "The Calcutta team is betting on quality, rather than quantity."

In the Coffee House, I could see perhaps two hundred boys (no girls) a very small percentage of the total population of Calcutta University (about 40,000 students). Sandy's hope, shared by the team, was that this intimate situation would produce in the long run good will for America more valuable than the massive approach of, say, the south India team.

There was a soft light cast over the room from the windows in the ceiling. Although Patti did not need flattering light, she looked particularly fresh and attractive in it. She wore no lipstick, but her hair had been cut recently by Mary Ann Buford and she was wearing a clean, starched print dress. Two hundred heads turned towards the door.

Patti, Lerner, and I walked in and sat down at an empty table. Before we had time to order, six college boys were crowded around us. Patti did not drink coffee, but one of the boys ordered it for her anyway. She let it grow cold before her as the talk began developing into a polite battle of wits.

Although the Indian boys may not have noticed, Patti bent over backwards to understand their point of view, even when she did not agree with it. She controlled herself and seemed never to forget that she was a guest in someone else's country. The Indian students, for that matter, were bending over backwards, too. As usual, they were friendly to a fault. No matter what they said, they began and ended with a smile. Even an avowed Communist student concluded a particularly acerb statement with "You are still my friend." In short, the Indian students never forgot that they were hosts.

In the next few days, I was able to eavesdrop on each member of Gram's team as the Coffee House hours wore on. I heard them talking philosophy, sports, politics, education, and sex. There was very little conscious humor and a great deal of teen-age profundity. Since Calcutta was the city in India subjected to the greatest volume of Communist propaganda, many of the questions asked by the Indians had a Red bias. There were more demands for admitting Red China to the U.N. and for putting a stop to atomic-bomb experiments. One boy wanted to know what we had done with Howard Fast, Paul Robeson, Charlie Chaplin, and the Rosenbergs, intoning those names as though they were sacred. There was a steady flow of adverse comment about America's position on Pakistan and Goa.

As in south India, American race relations were a constant souce of unhappiness and bewilderment for the Indian students. Mary Ann Buford bore the brunt of the questions on this score.

At George Wakiji's table, politics was less important than American education and American games. George simply was not politically minded. One boy reflected, though, that American students seem to have a great deal of time for extra-curricular activities, especially in the field of volunteer social service.

"They make time," George said.

"But most of our students," countered the boy, "are in need themselves and have no way of helping others."

In his quiet way George went about explaining how American students work their way through school. The boy shook his head in disbelief.

Bob Stein had a special attraction for the Indian students when they learned that his father was in the motion-picture business. They flooded him with questions about the private lives of American movie stars and the image of America created by our films. This discussion of films quite naturally brought forth such questions as: "Tell me, Bob, how many girls have *you* been intimate with?" And: "Does every date in the United States end in intercourse?"

Time after time the impact of American movies abroad was revealed to the Calcutta team not only in terms of morals, but also in questions of economics, social action, and politics. Usually our pictures had left an erroneous, if not downright harmful, impression—just as some bad Indian movies have done in America. Sandy Ragins, the team liberal, went so far as to suggest to me that the United States "really must do something about restricting movies sent overseas from America."

One afternoon I too became involved with a coffee-tableful of university students. Seven of us were sitting around a small glass-topped table, exchanging cigarettes and drinking coffee. They were a mild lot, not much interested in politics and the pursuit of power, but anxious to talk about Project India and the young people who made up the team.

One of them, a thin, graceful student named Banerjee, began asking some pointed questions about the project.

"How come you people don't have that famous American sense of humor, like your Mark Twain?"

"Well, we do," I said, "but we're here for a serious purpose, and most of the things we talk about aren't funny."

"We've all talked to you about American customs—marriage, for instance. That's funny, I think," Banerjee said, while his friends laughed. He went on: "In America, your men pick their wives; here they are picked for us and checked by the astrologer. In America, you marry the one you love. In India, you love the one you marry. Now isn't that funny?"

I could not tell, quite, whether Banerjee was making a bitter joke or a statement of fact. I intended to pursue his point, but Banerjee's friends erupted with a string of off-color stories, one more scatological than the next. So I waited until they finished.

At last, I was able to protest: "You won't hear any jokes from Project India; at least none like that."

"That's just what I mean," Banerjee said. "They're so sober all the time. Friendly, admirable, but sober."

"I don't think it's easy for optimistic, purposeful people like them to find things to make fun of," I said.

Another boy at the table, a fat, flat-lipped, jovial fellow named Roy, had been enjoying Banerjee's jibes and evidently felt that my rebuttal was rather weak.

"Do you mean that?" he shouted and cracked me on the arm, good-naturedly, but hard.

"Sure."

"No!" Roy said and whacked me again. I began to get annoyed.

"I say that people who represent their country abroad are often without humor—at least in public," I said.

"That may be true, Tom," Roy said, pronouncing my name with a long "o."

Then he laughed and hit me a third time, all in fun. My arm, I am sure, was already black and blue. I rolled up my shirt sleeve to have a look, and at the same time, I said: "I'd hate to spoil all the fine Indo-American relations that have been built up here, but if you hit me again—"

I was still half-kidding, but beginning to get angry, too.

The change that came over Roy was amazing. Suddenly I was his friend. There was respect between us. We knew where we stood. In the next week I saw Roy every day somewhere in Calcutta at a Project India function. By *not* being a jolly good fellow, I had apparently made a friend.

Young Banerjee also became a friend. One afternoon we met again at the Coffee House, and instead of staying, we went out for a walk.

"Did you ever hear of Harold Teen?" I asked him.

He had not.

"Well, Harold Teen was a comic strip character that was typical of a certain kind of American college man, and he used to hang around a place called the Sugar Bowl."

Banerjee waited patiently for the punch line.

"The India Coffee House reminds me of the Sugar Bowl. Neither one is very typical of college life."

"That is true," said Banerjee. "Most students do not go to the Coffee House. They cannot afford it."

I asked him if he thought Project India was spending too much time at the Coffee House. "I mean, maybe we'd be better off taking a nap in the afternoon instead of spending our time at the Coffee House."

Banerjee did not agree with me. I have tried to remember his exact words, but what follows is at best an accurate paraphrase.

"When Americans and Indians meet anywhere it can be a good thing," he said. "I admit that many of the boys at the Coffee House are frivolous boys. I admit that the United States can get along fine without bothering about them. And you will admit, I think, that India can get along without the California students. And it is true that in the Coffee House no one gets mad at anyone else, nor does one side make a joke about the other side. Few relationships last very long or are worth very much without some anger and some humor to test them and strengthen them. About the most that ever happens is that one of us says that Indians are more 'spiritual' than Americans, or one of you says that Americans are more 'practical' than Indians.

"But that is hardly an argument. Every man in the Coffee House would like to know what the California students know—that there is a job waiting for him when he gets out of school. Indians are as materialistic as anyone else. I have read about the American economy, about waste, and I am not so sure that Americans are as practical as they say they are. And I *know* that they are as spiritual as anyone else—for what that may be worth.

"So I have torn down just about everything the Coffee House visits with the California students is supposed to build. But can't we forget for a moment about Indians and Americans? If I have suggested that Americans and Indians have some differences, a great many similarities, and are all human beings, will you accept this? I mean, don't make me prove what is obvious."

I said I wouldn't make him prove it.

Banerjee took out an Indian cigarette, lit it, and held the match while I lit my American one. Then he continued:

"Suppose that someone in that Coffee House, American or Indian, after days and days of contact, begins to realize what we have just accepted as true, would you say that was beneficial?"

"Not particularly."

"Neither would I. But suppose he goes one step further and begins to realize that the admitted humanity of all peoples is not as great an idea as the wonderful differences in individuals. If he realizes that the most important being is the individual *as an individual* and not as a member of a family or a group or a nation or a race, then would you say the Coffee House hours were well-spent?"

I nodded. Banerjee at the age of twenty was making more sense, I thought, than some people make in a lifetime.

"Well," he said, "I have just told you what I learned in the Coffee House, not *from* the California students, but because they were *there*. I watched them and talked to them not once, but several times, and got a perspective. I do not think any of them even know me, but this is what I learned."

By this time our stroll had taken us back to the India Coffee House. Upstairs, the California students sat, each with a group of six or eight around him. I said goodbye to Banerjee and joined one of the groups, wondering if any of the American students were getting as much out of the Coffee House hours as Banerjee had.

15 WE WERE HAVING THE REGULAR BOILED LUNCHEON AT A LONG TABLE IN THE DINING ROOM OF THE RUSSELL HOTEL WHEN SANDY RAGINS ANNOUNCED PROJECT INDIA'S FINAL formal presentation before a Calcutta college assembly. It would be only their tenth performance in five weeks, a record far below that of the southern team, but a respectable record nevertheless, considering the differences in teams, audiences, and geography.

The Calcutta team did not have a Harold Otwell scheduling its presentations; Sandy Ragins had to make his own college dates, extracting promises and tentative dates from reluctant college principals without an introduction from U.S.I.S. Imagine yourself as one of six foreigners in, say, New York City, and think how many college presidents would suspend classes to hear you!

Neither did the Calcutta team have the advantage of being on the road with a schedule to be met; the college principals felt no pressure to arrange a student assembly on a particular date. Instead, the Calcutta team waited upon the principals' decisions, praying that somehow they would be able to make the best use of their time.

And because of the waiting, half of the presentations had to be crammed into their last full week in Calcutta, sandwiched between the work project at Santoshpur, Coffee House hours, and plans for a seminar. In that week, they appeared at the University Law College, Bangabasi, Central College, Javadpur College, and, finally, St. Xavier's College. When they went to the latter, Lerner and I went, too.

On the approach to St. Xavier's, I realized the greatest handicap of all: the campuses of Calcutta were hacked out of busy city blocks. There were no sweeping lawns and graceful driveways over which one could make a dramatic entrance—there were no passionate welcomes from a thousand cheering students and no sentimental farewells. They made their speeches, answered questions, and departed, quietly as they had come.

Patti Price made her opening speech on the stage at St. Xavier's before a packed assembly. She was in character: fresh, forthright, and vital. What she said about "why we have come to India" was not memorable, but how she said it—head up, chin out, hands clasped behind her back, feet together—probably convinced the audience that American girls are more independent and more worldly than their own.

George Wakiji followed Patti. When he talked, he held his back very straight and looked through his glasses over the heads of his audience. As in the Coffee House, he created a stir when he told them how he was working his way through school, and the boys' faces reflected many reactions: the desire to emulate, passing interest, and even dismay.

Mary Ann Buford, the team's other member from a "visible minority," followed George. Unlike Everett Brandon, Mary Ann did not have the knack of drawing on the feeling of racial mutuality between herself and the audience. Her speech pointed out that the homelife of a Negro in America was no different from the homelife of any other American. Where Everett was more inclined to appear before Indian audiences as a Negro, Mary Ann intended to appear as simply another American.

Bob Stein was perhaps closer to his audience's preconception of an American than any other member of the team. He was bland and self-confident. "American movies," Bob said, "are fantasies which entertain people for the simple reason that their stories *are* different from the normal everyday life of the people." Bob was making a sensible effort to counteract the millions of feet of film shipped every year from Hollywood to India. I do not think anyone believed him, but I thought he deserved credit for the effort.

Ron Pengilly followed Stein. His voice was comfortable, unhurried, and loud, but he could not get a response from his audience when he discussed student government. A responsible student movement in Calcutta, and elsewhere in India, was still a goal to be attained. In the meantime, the audience wanted to hear about national and international politics, which interested them far more than the political life of their own community or that of U.C.L.A.

Sandy Ragins was the anchor man of the Calcutta team. His corn-yellow hair and heavy glasses clashed on his head—the former emphasized his youth, the latter revealed the seriousness with which he looked upon life. He was conscious of his skill as an orator, and spoke now without his Bengali accent. His tack was religious freedom. He said that he planned to become a rabbi and spoke of the blessing of unrestricted worship as practiced in the United States and India. I thought Sandy's tack was somewhat misdirected. There was no anti-Semitism in India, no consciousness of anti-Semitism as a modern plague, and no desire to make any distinction at all between Jews, Christians, or Hindus. Thus, while Gram felt it necessary to have Catholic, Protestant, and Jewish representation on Project India, the Indians were not impressed one way or another. If there had been a Moslem American on the Project India team, that would have been a different matter. Sandy, however, was convinced that his point was not only accurate but also heavy with meaning. His talk disappointed me.

The question period followed. The boys of St. Xavier's posed the same questions as the boys and girls of south India, and the Calcutta team had essentially the same answers. I should point out, however, one exception:

A young Indian handed up a note on the issue of Goa. "How can we get the Portuguese out of our country?" he asked.

Ron Pengilly answered: "Violence will never do, and the Portuguese probably won't leave on their own accord, so why doesn't India *buy* Goa from Portugal?"

It struck me as a happy answer, but the audience made no response. For a moment there seemed to be a cold wind in the big room. Then the questioning continued, and the idea of buying Goa was forgotten.

At the end of an hour, Sandy lined up his team on the stage for a few songs. At least half of the Calcutta team could not carry a tune. Wisely, they sang two fast songs and closed the program with an off-key but sincere rendition of the Indian national anthem—which impressed the assemblage.

Finally, the group was led off stage to a series of classrooms where each member could answer more questions in more intimate circumstances. They had performed like a drill team during the presentation, and perhaps for that very reason their stage personalities lacked zest. In the classrooms, they were once again their old selves.

Sandy Ragins even resumed his fine Bengali accent in his ceaseless effort to make himself understood.

LATE one morning Patti Price held forth on the subject of American democracy as she stood in front of a left-wing bookstore. The store was right across the street from the University Law College. Her remarks were generally aimed at a handsome young Sikh whose beard had not yet reached maturity. A crowd quickly gathered, and what she said carried to a random selection of passers-by. I thought it was one of the most appealing scenes of the summer. Patti had a way of thrusting her chin up that made her look belligerent even when she was being agreeable. And the Sikh wore a most gentlemanly smile. I think he understood *her*, and that after all was the whole idea of Project India.

On another day I went with Ron Pengilly to an open-air tea room in a street near the University. Ron had heard about the place from a boy at the Coffee House.

"It's just a place where some students who never come to the Coffee House do their loafing," the boy had said.

Boldly, Ron went up to a very dark-skinned student, introduced himself, and started a conversation. Before long, the street was filled with young men and Ron was, in reality, holding a mass meeting. Most of the talk was about Goa. Independence Day (August 15th) was less than a week off and *satyagrahis* (non-violent demonstrators) from all over India were moving toward the Goa border for a *satyagraha* on that day. In the crowd around Ron, members of an organization called the Progressive Students Association were selling raffle tickets to raise money for half-a-dozen student *satyagrahis*. One boy offered to sell me a ticket, but I refused. I had the feeling that someone would probably get hurt on Independence Day and did not want to contribute.

In about thirty minutes, Ron shook hands with twenty or thirty students, said *"Namesthe"* to many more, and left the crowded street. It had been a minor interlude, but I was reasonably certain that the world would be a much more relaxed place to live in if more people from strange countries stood on street corners and talked to anyone who would listen.

Project India had still another point of contact with Indians and Indian life: now and again they were invited to dine at a student hostel or at a student's home. One of these invitations came from Manu Ojha, a tall, thin Brahman student with a handsome narrow face and a delicate mustache. His family was wealthy, religious, and strictly vegetarian. Manu lived in a four-story, U-shaped house, with a courtyard and gravel driveway in the "U" and broad terraces ringing each upper floor.

We met his family in the second-floor living room one evening just after dark. The room was large and crowded with chairs and sofas, a necessity when the family gathered because Manu's mother, fourteen brothers and sisters, and some sisters-in-law, nephews, and nieces all lived in the same house. The married couples, of course, had their own apartments on the upper floors.

Manu's father was dead, but his mother, a fine, fat woman with a look of absolute contentment on her face, was waiting in the living room to greet us. When we sat down, she passed around a small pamphlet, written in English, which related the wonderful life of the late Sri Ojha and included a listing of about twenty-five enterprises—lumbering, mining, shipping, steel, and the like—in which he had an interest before his untimely death. This may have been an immodest thing to do, but it did save us the trouble of asking a lot of questions.

Sandy Ragins and I were sitting on a soft divan directly beneath a ceiling fan. Manu sat on a chair next to Sandy. From that position, Manu introduced his brothers, sisters, sisters-in-law, nieces, and nephews as each made a brief appearance in the room. Manu told Sandy and me that a marriage had been arranged for him recently, but because the horoscope had not given a favorable report on the future, the contract had been broken.

We said we were sorry and turned our attention to the small talk in the room. The fan over head throbbed evenly. A particularly sweet odor hung in the air. Gram and Mrs. Ojha were talking about the weather, and Patti was talking about school to one of

Manu's brothers. The talk droned on and seemed to become part of the even beat of the fan. I was falling asleep. I dozed for a moment, and then snapped my head erect; I looked over at Sandy and saw that he was falling asleep, too.

It had been a long, hard day, beginning with Santoshpur early in the morning, and the pace was beginning to tell. Fortunately, neither of us dozed for very long, nor did we doze off at the same time, or else we would have been truly embarrassed. As it was, half asleep, I fell into an unnecessary argument with Manu.

Manu was talking about his faith in God. He said: "As a Brahman, ultimately I hope to find God—"

With no alert interest in what he was saying, I could only ask, "Why Manu?"

It was an innocent, drowsy question, but anger flared in Manu's refined, almond-shaped eyes, and he snapped back at me: "Because, when I find Him, I shall speak to Him!" He seemed astonished that I was not aware of this. "That should be the goal of every man's life—to prepare himself to talk with God."

"You mean *literally* speak to Him as I'm speaking to you?" I was wide awake now, but hopelessly involved.

"Of course!" he fairly shouted. He was very angry, and so was I. After all, he did not have to shout.

"Well," said I, walking off the deep end, "I'd say that shows great presumption on your part."

"*Talking to God?*" He did not believe his ears.

"I mean, Manu, who are *you?*"

From that moment on, Manu was no friend of mine, but I was spared the opportunity of making matters worse by the ringing of the dinner bell. I was sorry I had annoyed him, but the whole incident came as a complete surprise to me. I could not conceive that a college man would not want to argue about religion, but then I had never met anyone quite as religious as Manu.

Meals at Manu's house usually were served on the floor in the dining room, but with outsiders present the sacred eating place was not to be used. We walked upstairs to the third-floor terrace, where a long, narrow table had been set for the nine of us, Manu, his mother, and two of his brothers. At each place, there was a broad aluminum tray, a bottle of boiled water, and a towel. There were no utensils. We ate with our fingers.

Dinner was a juicy, spicy collection of curried vegetables, rice, and curd. For the second time in India, I thoroughly enjoyed the curry and decided eating it with my fingers even added something to its taste.

When we returned to the Russell Hotel, the manager was in a dither—Mary Ann Buford's cable call had come through at last and was waiting on the line from Los Angeles. It was Dennis, the boy friend.

"I'm fine," Mary Ann said. "How are you?"

They chatted for a minute or so, mostly about the set of matched luggage Dennis had given her, the weather, and when Mary Ann was coming home. When she hung up, Gram had an exasperated look in her eye.

"And I don't even like him," Mary Ann pleaded, but there was an unmistakable thrill in her voice. It was silly, but it was also a romantic thing for Dennis to do. I have often wondered whether Dennis followed up his advantage.

16 ON THE CALCUTTA TEAM'S LONG AND COMPLICATED SCHEDULE, ONE WEEK END WAS SET ASIDE FOR A VISIT TO FULIA, WHICH WAS A VILLAGE COMMUNITY DEVELOPMENT PROJect (C.D.P.) center seventy kilometers from the city. Late on a Friday night, they packed their overnight bags and resolved their doubts about the wisdom of the trip. Sandy Ragins argued that the team was in India to *teach* rather than to *learn* and should therefore spend Saturday and Sunday in Calcutta with Indian students. The others were unconvinced. They had heard so much about C.D.P. from the previous year's Project India team that they simply had to see for themselves. Gram Guenther let them fight it out. In the end, the majority prevailed, and next morning, in two cars provided by U.S.I.S., Sandy, Patti, Ron, Mary Ann, Bob, George, Lerner, and I drove out to Fulia.

I had expected to find more of what the southern team had seen at Panbkad, that silent, melancholy place near Ernakulam. But instead Fulia was something quite different—a compact little community of neat cottages, eight barn-sized buildings, and a dairy. And instead of ragged villagers, we were met by four well-dressed graduates of Calcutta University who were spending a month at Fulia to learn about C.D.P. They wore slacks and sport shirts and had the kind of intense passion for raising the villagers' standard of living that reminded one of the young men of the early New Deal. They spoke with unashamed adoration of the director of the Fulia C.D.P., a Mr. Sen, whom we were about to meet.

Mr. Sen came out of his cottage. He was a slim, wide-eyed man with heavy brows and black hair that lay flat on his skull. He wore a loose-hanging white gown and, except for that, looked very much like Eddie Cantor.

"*Namesthe*," he said and we all made the sign with our palms together. He shook hands with each of us and, before anything else, insisted that we take time to freshen up in cottages that had been assigned to Project India for the week end. Lerner and I explained that we two were returning to Calcutta that evening and tagged along with Patti and Mary Ann.

Inside, their cottage was like a nun's cell. It had bare walls and a bare floor, a night table and two beds. The place smelled anti-

138

septically clean and the corners of the room were still damp from a recent scrubbing. I sat on one of the beds. It was merely a slab of wood with four legs tacked on below and a coverlet spread out above. After the good springs and mattresses of the Russell Hotel, the girls were going to have a hard night.

In about ten minutes, one of the young University graduates came to lead us to a larger cottage, which was the central dining hall at Fulia. We were served tea and cashew nuts, while Mr. Sen and his aides conducted a brisk, business-like briefing on the Fulia C.D.P. Mr. Sen said:

"Among the villages of India, the primary necessity is rehabilitation. More than 300,000,000 people live in our villages, so the most important domestic need in India is rehabilitation. For agricultural rehabilitation, the villagers need irrigation and better tools. They need education in basic reading skills, basic information, and basic crafts. They need to increase productivity by learning to use more mechanical devices. But the people can only be moved up a step at a time. The workers develop their skills slowly. You do not jump a man from a handloom to a powerloom, but rather to the intermediate fly loom."

While he talked, Mr. Sen's hands fluttered gracefully before him. Ron, Patti, and George listened without taking their eyes off his face. Sandy scribbled a few notes, and Stein and Mary Ann only turned away from him to sip their tea. Mr. Sen continued:

"They need to develop artisans. This will lessen the pressure on the land. They need credit, short-term loans made available to them by the government, through a government agent, because private loans sometimes cost as much as fifty per cent per year in interest. And they need marketing assistance, too."

Mr. Sen's voice was very low, and its tone was confident. He did not have the slightest doubt that what was needed by the villagers would be forthcoming. But he never once used that imperial pronoun "we"; it was always the more modest "they." With proper assistance, they—the villagers—would do the developing themselves.

Finally, Mr. Sen said:

"All anyone is trying to do here is to carry out the philosophy of Gandhi, the hopes of the Five Year Plan, and the faith of people in America as well as those in India who have contributed so much to our community development."

Mr. Sen sat down, and a younger man took his place. "Now what *we* are trying to do here," he said, "is to change these villages over from subsistence farming to economic farming."

Holding up a large map, he rattled off the facts and figures of Fulia:

"Fulia is at the center of what we call a Development Block consisting of 113 villages in an area of 103 square miles. In the block there are 79,223 people, or about 800 to the square mile. This is more than the average, but not unusual.

"We have three health centers and three travelling medical units. We're selling a low-cost latrine for five rupees. We're trying to provide pure water to control dysentery and new procedures to control malaria. We've innoculated the people against typhoid, smallpox, and cholera. While you Americans have been in Calcutta, there has been a serious cholera epidemic, but it has not spread here. We're offering maternity care and child welfare services. . . ."

The man droned on, managing to make the exciting, impressive accomplishments of Fulia seem commonplace. Yet the California students could visualize hundreds of development blocks all over India and begin to see why the Indians had hope for the future.

According to one estimate, however, India's population in 2005 would be 840,000,000—they would need all the hope they could get.

After the briefing session, Mr. Sen led the Americans on a tour of a polytechnical institute which was housed in the big buildings at Fulia. Sandy Ragins walked next to him while the others followed close behind with the younger C.D.P. workers. They met barefooted teen-age boys and girls, fresh from back-country villages, learning foundry work, tool making, printing, sewing, and painting in the various buildings. Four out of five of these young craftsmen could look forward to steady jobs upon leaving the institute. Then, at the Fulia dairy, Mr. Sen introduced his guests to men who a few years before had known nothing but back-breaking work in the rice fields. Now these men operated a modern, sanitary pasteurizing plant as though they had known machinery all their lives.

After lunch, Mr. Sen arranged for us to inspect neighboring villages. Sandy, Ron, George, and Bob Stein went off in a truck with a group of C.D.P. officials while Patti, Mary Ann, Lerner, and I climbed into a jeep with seven other people. One of our companions was a young man called the Gram Sewak, who had been trained by the government to teach new skills and techniques to the villagers. His female counterpart, the Gram Sewika, came with us, too, along with two young girls from one of the villages we were to visit. Besides, there were two C.D.P. officials, and the driver of the jeep in which the eleven of us would ride. All but the two officials were squeezed inside the jeep. The officials rode on the hood, hanging on for dear life as we raced down the road.

Four miles later, we turned off the paved highway onto a narrow, deeply rutted country road that seemed to lead directly into a dense green jungle. A turn appeared further on, however, and we found ourselves driving through a ghost town. On both sides of the road, there were empty houses and temples, boarded up and overgrown with moss. The grass in the yards grew higher than the window sills. We made another turn and suddenly, we were in the center of the shrunken, but still lively village of Habibpur.

In the past two hundred years, the Ganges, which used to run nearby, had changed its course, and Habibpur had been reduced from a bustling river town to a bustling village. It was still the center of an agricultural area, the marketplace for seven smaller villages that surrounded it. Taken together, these eight villages were the bailiwick of the Gram Sewak and the Gram Sewika.

The village people gathered around our jeep and began to laugh as we piled out; they had never seen a jeep with so many people in it. We followed the Gram Sewak into a weather-beaten stone building that had bars on the windows, but no door. In better days, it might have been the Habibpur jail, but now it was the local C.D.P. headquarters.

The Gram Sewak was a tall quiet man wearing a *dhoti* and shoes. He carried a big black umbrella. He smiled at us and began speaking Hindi, pointing at marks on a large map with the tip-end of his umbrella. Not knowing how to tell us he did not speak English, he simply did what he thought he ought to do—show us where we were. Fortunately, one of the Fulia officials spoke our language and translated for us.

Patti Price studied the Gram Sewak's map like an explorer. She asked about inter-village communications, rate of crop failures, monsoon rainfall, and the local diet. And then she was shocked when the Gram Sewika suggested that the American girls come with her to visit some homes in Habibpur, while the Gram Sewak took Lerner and me on a tour of the real back-country. Before Patti rebelled openly, I explained that we might learn more if all of us stayed together. It didn't make sense, but everyone agreed then that the girls should accompany us.

We walked three miles down a muddy road between a tangled green forest and a tall stand of rice. The road, we learned, was quite new, having been opened for the first time only two years before, while the village toward which we were going was nearly three hundred years old. The name of the village was Kalaighata.

It was a sharecroppers' village on the edge of a jute field; and seemed to be the poorest place in India. The huts had no walls— only floors, side-poles, and roofs without chimneys. Each floor was four feet thick, made of cow dung and mud. Living that high off the ground, the villagers *hoped* to be safe from snakes, vermin, and flood waters. A few roofs were made of tile, but most of them were thatched with palm leaves.

In one hut a woman was cooking, while her husband and the children stood quietly outside. Smoke poured from under the eaves. One of our guides told us that with the help of an American Point Four technician who had recently been in the vicinity, the principles of chimneys and chimney-building were being taught. He was hopeful that Kalaighata's husbands and children would soon be able to stay indoors when dinner was being cooked.

Only a third of Kalaighata's two hundred people were bold enough to reveal themselves to us. The toothless chief of the village greeted us with a friendly "*Namesthe.*" When the Gram Sewak asked him to show Patti and Mary Ann the new rugs woven by the village women, the old man grinned shyly and seemed about to refuse. But after more talk, he overcame his embarrassment and ordered the rugs brought forward. These were the simplest kind of palm-frond mat. A village woman could weave one in a week and earn two rupees for it in the marketplace at Habibpur. Patti pored over the mats; she fingered them, pulled them, and tested their strength.

"I wish I could do that!" she said.

Patti's wish was translated for the chief. He issued another command and, instantly, two mats were spread on the ground about ten yards apart. A child brought a basket of palm fronds and dumped them in the center of one mat, and six village women sat down around the pile, leaving a place in their circle for Patti and Mary Ann to join them and learn. The second mat was for the Gram Sewak, the chief, the village snake charmer, Lerner, and me—the men, it seemed, would rest while the women worked; so we sat down and smoked.

Through our interpreter, the Gram Sewak explained that he had been working for two years in Kalaighata. Since then, he had taught every adult in the village to write his own name, while the Gram Sewika had taught the women to weave mats. The money received for the mats was not as important, he said, as the sense of pride that came from creative work.

While Patti and Mary Ann bent over their weaving, more villagers dared come have a look at us, especially a large group of naked children with swollen bellies and diseased eyes.

The snake charmer, a rail-thin, tattooed man with a proud record of cured patients, showed me the mirror that he used to draw out the poison from snake bite wounds. He was a good-humored snake charmer, but very serious about his profession.

I asked the interpreter if the people of Kalaighata had knowledge of the outside world. He assured me that they did, that information is passed around by word-of-mouth. On an impulse, I turned to the chief and asked him if he had ever heard of Russia. There was a pause for translation, then the shy old man shook his head. Negative.

"China?" I asked.

Negative.

"U.S.A.?"

He nodded and said something to this effect:

"The U.S.A. gives us milk!"

The interpreter explained that the village had received powdered milk from Omaha, Nebraska, and that the letters U.S.A. had been clearly stamped on the side of the box.

At this point, Patti, with a triumphant toss of her head, held aloft a section of matting, one-foot square, which she had successfully woven under the tutelage of the village women. All the women were smiling at her, covering their mouths with their hands to hide their ugly teeth.

It was time to move on, but the chief insisted that before leaving we must see the pride of his village, a banyan tree on the shores of the Churni River, which flowed and sometimes overflowed a few hundred yards from the center of the village.

By now the girls' sneakers were caked with mud. Patti had unconsciously rubbed a dirty hand across her cheek, leaving a smudge the size of a silver dollar. Both were dead tired from the long hike to Kalaighata and from the thought of having to walk all the way back again. But duty called, and they joined the vanguard heading for Kalaighata's tree. Overhead, two giant vultures patrolled the sky.

The banyan tree was huge: it had eight trunks stuck in the ground and a dozen more limbs reaching hungrily for the earth. The central, original trunk was perhaps twenty feet in circumference. Some of the limbs had taken root in the ground and were almost as large. You had the feeling that if the banyan tree was left to grow forever, it would someday cover the earth. Moreover, it was cool beneath its leaves. No wonder the people of Kalaighata were proud of their tree.

A country boat pulled into the shore just then, and a boatman offered to take us for a ride on the Churni River, a narrow stream that was nearly clogged with water-lily pads. He chattered with our interpreter, who then told us a local legend.

In the days when the Churni was part of the mighty Ganges River system, the British general, Clive, had escaped across it at night after his armies had been defeated in the north. The people of the village protected him and led him to safety, and thereafter the name of their village was Kalaighata (Clive's steps?) in honor of the man they saved.

The story may not be true, but if you listen carefully, I believe you can hear Clive's name in "Kalai."

After hearing that story, we had to take a ride on the Churni River. The boatman poled us upstream for ten minutes, then let us float down again to the banyan tree landing. Patti and Mary Ann poured out their thanks, not only to the boatman, but to the chief of the village, the Gram Sewak and the Gram Sewika, and anyone else they could find. Then with a sigh of profound resignation, they set off on the muddy road for Habibpur. Fortunately, the jeep driver had driven in through the muck to Kalaighata, and we did not have to walk after all.

Back in Habibpur, we saw things now that we had not noticed before. The homes had walls and chimneys; the main street was overrun with cows, goats, and dogs; the children looked healthier than their neighbors. The men and women in Habibpur must have been literate because there were posters on some of the walls. Their handicrafts were more intricate and their social life seemed more diverse.

The Gram Sewika had been teaching the women the art of food preservation. They came for instruction to the Habibpur Social Education Center, which was merely a mat on the ground, four poles and a roof. It had no sidewalls, but it was still the first community center in Habibpur's history. Its chief significance was in the people who came to it—women who never before had been away from their own neighborhoods, men who had never before organized themselves in order to learn, and children who could at least hope for a better life than that of their parents.

Patti and Mary Ann understood—both girls were tired, dirty, hot, and thirsty, but they flung themselves onto the mat and raved over the handiwork of local women which was displayed before them.

Near sundown, we dragged ourselves back to Fulia where a U.S.I.S. car was on hand to take Lerner and me back to Calcutta.

Mr. Sen accompanied us in the gloom to our car. I told him I had enjoyed the day and added that the C.D.P. was one of the most hopeful things I had seen in India. In his soft way, Mr. Sen thanked us for coming and shook hands, Western-style.

Through the dark countryside, the U.S.I.S. driver drove at a comfortable speed, around trucks loaded with produce for the Calcutta market and farmers getting home late from the jute fields. Lerner and I smoked and talked until, quite without warning, Calcutta burst upon us. It was Saturday night and the big town was going full blast; its streets had never seemed so crowded.

In the middle of this chaotic nightlife we saw a decrepit old man squatting impassively on the sidewalk. He had made a stove out of a tin can and held a piece of meat over the opening. With a newspaper, he fanned mightily until smoke billowed up in great, blooming clouds that enshrouded the shops and strollers nearby. The old man did not care. He kept on fanning, and the smoke thickened until it looked like white foam. He was soon lost from sight, but for blocks afterward, I could still see his smoke rising in thick white folds.

At our hotel, we learned that Gram was spending the night with Jane Fairweather, the U.S.I.S. Librarian in Calcutta. Miss Fairweather's bedroom was air-conditioned, I'd heard, and I was glad that Gram was getting a chance to escape, if only for one night. Gram had left a message telling us she had heard from Bob Jaffie. His southern team was on its way north by train from Guntur. They would arrive Monday morning—in time for the Calcutta team's all important seminar, which was next on the schedule.

Lerner and I cleaned up and went to Firpo's, a plushy restaurant on Chowringhee Road. The maitre d'hotel sent us back once to fetch our jackets, but even he could not dampen our spirits. In spite of him we had a steak dinner, listened to the music of a New Zealand jazz band, and enjoyed our first free night in weeks.

17 IMAGINE FOURTEEN PEOPLE IN A SINGLE EMBRACE! THIS WAS THE SCENE IN THE BACKYARD OF THE RUSSELL HOTEL WHEN THE TWO TEAMS OF PROJECT INDIA WERE REUNITED. It was raining, but no one minded that. They shouted for joy, kissed each other, and wrung hands until they were arm weary. The southern team—Ed Peck, Jerry Lewis, Everett Brandon, Ruth Taketaya, Rosemary Wooldridge, Joe Michels, and Bob Jaffie—was on time and in good health. After they had been assigned rooms, they crowded into Gram's parlor to find out about the two-day seminar scheduled to start that very afternoon.

Sandy Ragins, they learned, was chairman of a committee composed of nine Indian students plus the Calcutta team. The committee had held meetings eighteen times in the past month to organize the seminar. The students had shared expenses, planned a program, ordered invitations, and arranged for a hall. They had made all their plans on a strict majority-rule basis. For a theme, they had selected "The Student's Responsibilities in Life," with individual seminars on three sub-topics: "The Responsibilities of the Student to the Past," "The Responsibilities of the Student to the Present," and "The Responsibilities of the Student to the Future."

Sandy Ragins and two Indian students were to be chairmen of the seminar. Scottish Church College, a block off College Street, had donated an auditorium and classroom space from 4:30 P.M. to 8:00 P.M. for the first day, and from 3:15 P.M. to 8:00 P.M. for the second day. Every college in the Calcutta area had received an invitation asking them to send two delegates to the seminar.

When it was over, the final count showed that forty colleges had been represented, including one situated more than a hundred miles from Calcutta. The final session, held from 7:00 P.M. to 8:00 P.M. on the last evening, was declared an open meeting and over four hundred students attended.

From beginning to end, the Calcutta team coordinated all the activities and attended to the smallest details, even to borrowing an American flag and an Indian flag for the opening and closing sessions of the seminar.

147

To get to Scottish Church College, you take the double-deck bus from Chowringhee and Park and get off at the reservoir on College Street, which is about a mile beyond the India Coffee House. The reservoir is one of Calcutta's favorite swimming pools. It is directly in front of Scottish Church College. Outside the College, while the seminar was going on, the swimming pool was crowded with people, like the Y.M.C.A. pool back home on Saturday afternoon. Even in the College auditorium, you could hear the shouts of young men playing water polo, the dull smack of the ball on the water, and the cries of vendors who sold sweetmeats and soft drinks to people up on the grass.

In short, while Project India and a group of Indian students conducted their round-table discussions, life went on—and death, too. In front of the College on the second night, a dead man lay on his bier, covered with red and white flowers, waiting to be hoisted aloft by his pallbearers and carried to the burning ghats along the sacred river.

By 5:00 P.M. on the first day, registration was complete and the introductory session of the seminar got under way. In the dimly lit Scottish Church College auditorium, there were close to a hundred people. Each one held a mimeographed copy of the seminar program. At the top of the program were two quotations. One was from Gandhi:

"The very right to live accrues to us only when we do the duty of citizenship of the world.

"A man is but the product of his thoughts; what he thinks, that he becomes."

The second quotation was from Lincoln:

". . . we shall remember, while we exercise our opinion, that others have also rights to the exercise of their opinions, and that we should endeavor to allow those rights, and act in such a manner as to create no bad feeling."

I thought that they could have found something better than that prissy quotation in all the writings of Abraham Lincoln, but it *was* appropriate in its way because of Sandy's intense desire that the seminar should remain a seminar and not develop into a debating exercise for a few boys. The Indian students had vast experience in debate and almost none in the seminar type of discussion. The round-table was new to most of them and perhaps aggravating to some. But the California students were determined to present their method of testing ideas and reaching agreements through the seminar technique. It was a complex undertaking. I do not believe it could have been organized and carried out without someone like Sandy Ragins working at the center of things. The seminar was his great feat of the summer and easily the single most important contribution to the success of the project in Calcutta.

The keynote address was delivered by "Robert Jaffie, educator from Burbank, California." The loudspeaker system was working poorly, and momentarily I thought the seminar was about to fail without having had half a chance. But Jaffie kept talking, and the Indian students seemed to like what they heard. They applauded enthusiastically and then divided themselves into groups for the seminar, according to their interest in the past, present, or future.

Lerner and I first briefly attended the seminar on the present, which was held in the college library. About twenty-five boys and girls ranged themselves behind four long tables, which unfortunately could not be moved into a complete square. The library was not well designed acoustically, and the distance separating the speakers made hearing even more difficult. Moreover, Sandy had given orders that the "feel" of a discussion should be maintained at all times. This meant that the students would speak sitting down.

Thus handicapped, the discussion began, with Ron Pengilly and Mary Ann Buford in the room representing the Calcutta team. The chairman of the seminar was a somewhat indecisive young man named Morwah. He announced that the seminar would cover three areas of present-day student responsibility—to the university, to the community, and to political life. The program called for brief speeches by two students of Calcutta University and by Ron and Mary Ann, followed by a general discussion among the group. The first speaker was Odero-Jowi, an exchange student from Kenya, a jet-black African with a resonant voice. He talked much too long and not always on the subject, but it was a pleasure to hear him speak so beautifully.

Mary Ann spoke second. For about four minutes, she talked along this line: "Students must learn self-restraint," she said, "and how to live in the present-day world without outside discipline."

So far so good, but lacking a strong chairman, this seminar promised to develop very slowly. So Lerner and I crept out of the library, crossed through the auditorium where Gram and Jaffie were sitting with their heads together exchanging experiences, and entered a lecture hall on the far side of the hall.

Here Sandy Ragins was moderating "responsibilities to the past." His seminar group was not as large as the one we had left. The past, it seemed, was not quite so exciting to the Indian students as the present and the future. Sandy sat at the base of the lectern, facing about fifteen boys and girls. They were sitting on the front row benches of an ascending tier. With George Wakiji and two Calcutta University students, Sandy was to start things off by discussing the cultural and socio-economic background of the student, but by the time I had arrived, Lata Roy, the girl who had given me a friendship bracelet at Santoshpur, had taken command of the meeting.

Lata was a plump girl with clear-plastic rimmed glasses. Standing beneath the one bare bulb which lighted the room, she wore a lovely green, white, and red sari that made one forget the drabness and the gloom of that cavernous room. I really had not understood what the phrase "responsibilities to the past" was all about. But listening to Lata, I began to see; it was a phrase of deep significance to her and to many young Indians.

She was saying: "Let me tell you, our friends from America, what academic training, the accumulation of the wisdom of the past, does for us. It makes us fit for *unemployment*. No, there is nothing exciting about the British style of education we are getting here in Calcutta. It only means we get no jobs when we graduate. The really exciting thing in Indian education today is what the Gram Sewaks and the Gram Sewikas are teaching people in the villages. It is not here."

Lata did not sit down, but a boy at the far end of the front row raised his hand, and Sandy pointed a pencil at him. The boy stood up.

"You don't have to stand unless you want to," Sandy told him.

The boy stood, hands in his pockets, his body leaning a bit sideways. It was a new experience for him to be speaking in public, and he was determined to stand. He said:

"The difference between education in America and education in India is simply this—American students learn about the past, but we Indians are forced to live in it. We cannot escape it. Our villages, some of them, are almost as far into the past as you can go. I say that the question here is whether our past should be a chain that binds us or a guidepost that directs us." The boy sat down, flushing happily.

Lata Roy answered him:

"Well, it seems to me that there is a race in India today between ambition and tradition. I admit that, since Independence, our ambitions have been winning a few victories. Sometimes I think the past is not *quite* so much with us now. At least, I can say that our cities are free. And even our villages are changing. At long last, they are developing *the questioning mind.*"

Lata spoke her last sentence almost desperately. The villagers were her brothers. She could not thrust them from her mind. They represented her roots. They must be lifted up before India could take real pride in itself.

Listening to Lata, I recognized a profound difference between her and, say, Sandy Ragins or Patti Price or Everett Brandon. Lata had deep roots and little pride. The Americans had few, if any, roots and pride to burn. Lata need only drive out to Fulia and she knew she would find her brothers living near the rock-bottom of existence. Sandy, Patti, or Everett were from California where rootlessness is a cliché. It was their luck to be born where there were no limits on pride; in America there was nothing between them and their own visions of the future; they were born full-grown into wide-open country, while Lata was born knowing that to discourage snakes, vermin, and flood waters, her brothers still live four feet off the ground seventy kilometers from Calcutta.

The Californians had no sense of limitations, no clear idea of the possible and the impossible—not knowing from what common root they came, they acknowledged no limits as to how high they could go. They had come to India for just this reason. Lata Roy would never think of going to America to make friends for India. There was the difference. The Americans were the wanderers, the seekers.

Perhaps, I thought, "rootlessness" had a value all its own. It was a primary source of creative power in America. Those who urge the young generation nowadays to sink its roots in a specific culture may be asking them to give up too much.

Lata Roy did not speak again that evening, and I lost interest, although the discussion under Sandy's guidance waxed eloquently for an hour or more. I did not take another note on the seminar until the next afternoon when I visited the third seminar session, which concerned itself with the future. Patti Price and Bob Stein were the Calcutta team's representatives, but Patti was doing most of the talking now. Her prime opponent was a well-dressed older student, A. C. Bose, chairman of the meeting and, with Sandy Ragins, a chairman of the seminar itself. Bose was a brilliant young man, but a poor moderator. Instead of utilizing Patti as a stimulus for discussion among the other twenty people in the classroom, he encouraged *her* to talk. The session thus became a question-and-answer period, with the answers largely provided by Patti. The repartee went like this:

A: "Don't you think progress needs an ideological basis?"

Patti: "I think you can be a realist and still have ideals that lift your goals."

B: "What is the American ideology?"

Patti: "Well, we believe in a government of laws, not men; in freedom; in equality."

C: "Inequality?" (Very Shocked.)

Patti: "Equality."

Later on, the moderator himself joined the discussion, which by then had reached the A-bomb. Ed Peck was seated on one of the lower benches and involved himself in it.

Bose: "I say there is reason to fear radiation from an atomic test."

A very indignant Peck: "Radioactive fallout is a myth. There is less radiation after an atomic blast in Nevada than there is in a wrist watch that glows in the dark."

Obviously, the seminar was not an uninterrupted flow of brilliance, communication, and understanding.

But the basic goal was realized. The Indian students were enthused by the idea of the seminar. Americans and Indians had cooperated on a common project with rare success. And the final session was perhaps the most striking of all. Dr. H. C. Mukherjee, the Governor of West Bengal, and Dr. N. K. Siddhanta, the Vice-Chancellor of Calcutta University (whose title is equivalent to President of an American university) both spoke at the final meeting before four hundred Indian and Californian students. The notes of the seminars had been rushed to Dr. Siddhanta at 5:30 P.M. so that he might appear at 7:00 P.M. with an intelligent idea of what had been discussed. He had read the notes; his speech was based in every detail on the collected sentiments of the seminar's participants. He made a unity out of the student's responsibilities to past, present, and future. Dr. Siddhanta said:

"In the past, the temporal things are really more important to our study than the permanent things. In the present, we must distinguish between information, knowledge, and wisdom. Considering our future, we cannot know the world until we know our own country. I say that the fine thing about this seminar was the spirit of it. Mutual work. Democratic discussion. Thinking."

He gave a good, grave speech, convincing both the Indian students and the Americans that with all its shortcomings, the seminar had been a meaningful experience for them. He gave the seminar concrete value.

Sandy Ragins never felt better or more relieved in his life. He had done his job well, and now it was all over except for one final act. Proudly, he stepped to the microphone and, turning to the Vice-Chancellor, said:

"May I give you this check for three thousand rupees to help

needy students at Calcutta University." Sandy reached for the
envelope worth about six hundred dollars. "This money was raised
by last year's Project India team," he continued, "from its speaking
engagements and fund-raising activities in California."

Everything was fine, except that there was no check in the envelope. It was lost!

With good grace, the Vice-Chancellor accepted the gift that
wasn't there. After the meeting, which closed with the singing
of "The Star Spangled Banner" and "Janaganamana," the Indian
national anthem, the check was found in a book where it had been
placed for safe-keeping, and another good deed was done.

Afterward, Ron Pengilly summed up what was—for me, at
least—the great revelation of the seminar.

"One thing that impressed me," Ron said, "was the attitude of
Indian women. At the seminar, the boys rambled all over the place,
while the girls stuck to the point and had something to say. The
boys wanted to solve their problems by founding an All-India
Student Union, but the girls wanted to go to work in their own
college community. I'd say that it would be good for India if
there was more real coeducation, if the girls had more chances to
make themselves heard. . . ."

18 THE FIRST NIGHT PROJECT INDIA'S SOUTHERN TEAM WAS IN CALCUTTA, ALL SIXTEEN OF US WERE INVITED TO DINNER BY JANE FAIRWEATHER, THE U.S.I.S. LIBRARIAN. MISS FAIR-weather was a plump affectionate woman who lived on one of the upper floors of an American-owned apartment house. Her place was elegantly furnished with a combination of American furniture and Indian objets d'art, which she had collected during her years abroad. The dinner had the same international flavor, but its most welcome item was *filet mignon*.

After dinner the teams sang songs which they had written in spare moments during the past week at the Russell Hotel and on the long train ride north from Guntur. The tunes were old, but the lyrics were new and designed to poke fun at everyone; even Lerner and I came in for our share of the ribbing. When the singing ended, Gram Guenther and Bob Jaffie exchanged seats—symbolically exchanging leadership of the two teams. For the rest of the summer, Gram would lead Ed Peck's group and Jaffie would lead Sandy Ragins'.

The shank of the evening was given over to reminiscences. Sandy Ragins told a story I had not heard before. It seemed that a few days after his team arrived in Calcutta, the four boys had gone off in search of some real Indian Communists—not the student variety. Innocently, they asked directions and finally walked into what they thought was an everyday Communist meeting place. Instead, they found themselves staring into the astonished face of a *Chinese* Communist, in *his* Calcutta headquarters. On both sides, there was an awful moment of recognition. Then the boys backed out of the door while the bewildered Chinese attempted to load them up with literature from "new" China. When word of the incident spread to the American consulate, the California students were called into U.S.I.S. for a scolding, and then nothing more was said about it.

Around midnight, we left Jane Fairweather's and walked back to the Russell Hotel. The southern team, Lerner, and I were able to go right to bed, but the Calcutta team was not so fortunate. They not only had to prepare for the second session of the seminar coming up on the next afternoon, but they also had to get ready for a summing-up session scheduled for 10:00 in the morning at the United States Information Service. It was to be a round-table meeting with the four top officers of U.S.I.S., and Gram wanted the team to be primed for it.

When Lerner and I had arrived in Calcutta, we had visited U.S.I.S. on our second day in town, bearing Harold Otwell's regards from Trivandrum and desperate for a look at *The New York Times*. First we met Aileen Aderton, the cultural affairs officer, and then Jane Fairweather. In contrast to Miss Fairweather, Miss Aderton was thin and not so gay, but both women impressed us with their perspective on four years of Project India.

That same morning at U.S.I.S., we met Thomas Needham, the Public Affairs Officer and top executive of U.S.I.S. in Calcutta. Needham was a barrel-chested man who had been in the public relations business before entering government service. In turn, he introduced us to his information officer, Glen Smith, a thin, blond, intense ex-newspaperman.

I did not get to know them too well in Calcutta, but these were . the four people seated across from Gram, Jaffie, and the twelve California students at the summing-up session next morning. We were in Needham's office, a pale green room equipped with standard U.S. Government office furniture.

Sandy Ragins began with a report on the team's accomplishments in five weeks of work in Calcutta. It reflected their single-minded devotion to hard work—their eagerness to succeed and, if possible, make a better showing than any other Project India team. The four U.S.I.S. officials listened quietly. I found myself wishing that Sandy had been less formal about his report. Once he had given me a summing-up in three sentences that was more to the point:

"In a crude sense, we're in a propaganda fight," Sandy had explained. "But beyond that, something important has been proved. We've shown that work can be done together by Indians and Americans."

After Sandy, Ron, George, Bob, and Mary Ann made supplementary reports, Patti Price summarized the problem of communicating with Indian students—especially those who think the international edition of *Time* magazine represents American opinion and who, on the other hand, listen daily to a steady barrage of Communist propaganda.

The total impression of their report was that they had worked every minute of every day for five weeks, and, indeed, that was very nearly the truth. Needham mulled over that impression. He lit a cigarette and dropped the lighted match into a water-filled ashtray on his desk; the match sizzled when it hit the water. Then, he said:

"Don't misunderstand me. I think, for instance, that your seminar is a grand idea. But don't you think that as each Project India group becomes more efficient, learning each year from the experiences and mistakes of the previous teams, that there will be less and less time for the group itself to be affected by the experience?"

Gram answered: "It's true that last year's team passed on a lot of experiences, but they also enabled these people to build on their friendships. To me, it is the friendships that are most important."

Needham continued: "I think this group was and is continuing to be an important group. You are setting a pattern. Other colleges will hear about Project India and will imitate it. Good or bad, you are setting the course for these groups, and that's why I don't want to see the thing spoil or collapse under its own weight."

Glen Smith, the information officer, had been listening intently. He, too, seemed very grave, saying, "What is really important and what will really make you successful is that you will ably and maturely present to people back home what they look like to an Indian, what they look like to people abroad. Now, you have to take the time to find out what these people are thinking. Just being busy isn't success."

Aileen Aderton, the cultural affairs officer, had still another idea: "I wonder if the Project India groups are developing, over the years, too much self-assurance and are losing the knack of self-questioning among themselves? This year's team, working alone and in pairs much of the time, seems so much more independent than last year's team."

Patti replied, "We warn ourselves every day that we must not take the Indian kids for granted. We try to keep away from thinking in stereotypes. We constantly ask ourselves whether it is better to see lots of students, like the southern team did, or just get to know a few. We've constantly had the old argument among ourselves about quantity versus quality."

Needham smiled at Patti. "Well, you must cope with that argument every day of your life on the basis of your experience, intelligence, and intuition. Partly by choice and partly by budget, we cope with the same situation here at U.S.I.S. The Reds try to spread propaganda to Indian people on a mass, saturation-attack basis. The U.S.I.S. tries to give the facts to those who lead the opinions of others."

Ten minutes later, as we were leaving, Glen Smith had one more thing to say: "What amazes me is the way, year after year, Project India teams are selected by Miss Guenther way back in California and yet, four years in a row, the teams have been better than good. Every one of the kids has had courage, dignity, poise, and intelligence. It's a fine record."

PROJECT India's work in Calcutta ended next day. The sixteen of us checked out of the Russell Hotel and rode to Howrah Station in a caravan of taxis. We were taking the night train south to Puri, a resort town on the Bay of Bengal where for three days the California students were to rest, reflect, and—for a change—talk only to each other.

Howrah was busier than Grand Central Terminal on a Friday afternoon. Refugees, porters, vendors, and passengers surged in every direction across its inner plaza. Deftly, Jaffie led us through the proper gate and we found our railroad car about halfway down the platform. I had thought we were through with Calcutta University students for a while, but a crowd of two hundred of them were on hand for a rousing send-off. One young man presented Sandy Ragins with a golden bouquet of flowers. Sandy flushed red from his chin to his eyebrows and threw his free arm around the shoulder of his friend. Each of us had our own private cluster of well-wishers, acquaintances, and chums. A Nepalese boy whom I had met at Santoshpur even asked me to spend a week with him in Katmandu before returning to America.

Of course it was impossible, but how I regret not having gone with him!

All around me, the handshaking and embracing reached new peaks of good fellowship. The Indian students obviously had deep feelings for the Calcutta team, but they did not discriminate against the southern team, either. No one left Howrah Station without the Big Good-by.

At last the train bell rang. Our luggage was aboard, but there was still the problem of squeezing ourselves through the crowd into the compartments. On the way to the door, I had to stop again and again to sign autograph books, "Greetings from U.S.A., your friend, Tom Morgan." At last Lerner grabbed my hand and pulled me up into our two-man compartment as the train began to move out. For Lerner and me, it was our final crowd of students. After Puri, we would return to Calcutta and from there fly to Bombay and Europe, while Project India spent another three weeks on the sub-continent.

19 THE BEAUTIFUL BUFF-COLORED BEACH AT PURI, WASHED CLEAN BY THE WARM WATERS OF THE BAY OF BENGAL, WAS AN IDEAL RESTING-AND-REFLECTING PLACE FOR THE California students. The soft sand and foaming water were soothing to minds too long on the alert and feet too long in Western shoes. The fishermen who trolled near the shore with long, heavy nets worked so effortlessly that they had a calming influence on all who watched them. Their fishing boats were mere logs, tiny kayaks without cockpits bobbing on the surf. Wearing white pointed straw hats, they straddled the logs, dangled their legs in the water for balance and propulsion, and rode back and forth on the rhythmic cross-currents.

For complete relaxation, the students sat on the upstairs patio of the Eastern Railway Hotel in big wicker chairs with their feet up and for hours just looked at the sky, the blue water, and that vast, empty strip of sand.

On the first night there, they built a bonfire on the beach. They sang many songs, but as Bob Stein said:

"We have a beach party with a fire and everything, just like back home. Only how many beach parties have you gone to where the kids sang 'God Bless America' and 'America, The Beautiful'?"

Over and over, I heard the California students say that in India they were rediscovering America.

"I've become quite a patriot since I left home," admitted Sandy Ragins, who could be expected to be a stern critic and dissenter when he was actually back there. "I see real physical and spiritual strength in America that I never saw before."

"You develop a lot of patriotism in a short time," Bob Stein said. "There's a lot right at home that we take for granted."

"Let me tell you one thing I've come away with," said George Wakiji. "I've been fortunate myself, being a man of two cultures, but India has wised me up about America. It is more than material things—it's something else we have, and we all ought to think twice before knocking America because of it."

The songs they sang around the fire on the beach were part of this pattern. Gram Guenther had said on several occasions that the personal experiences of the students were secondary to their

163

main goal: the creation of understanding of Americans in India.
But at Puri, Bob Jaffie said to me:

"Gram will tell you she doesn't raise $25,000 from the Ford
Foundation people just to provide a liberal education and travel
for twelve U.C.L.A. students, but I say you can't draw the line
in deciding the value of Project India. There are simply two
beneficial results—Indians learn something about America, Americans learn something about India. And of course, in the process,
they both learn something about themselves."

NEXT day, Lerner and I sought out Patti Price. Lerner wanted to
photograph her against some of the more exotic backgrounds of
Puri. We found her on the upstairs patio getting a haircut from
Ruth Taketaya, but she agreed to come along with us as soon
as Ruth was finished. We sat down to wait.

"I still feel like I'm walking through a newsreel or the pages of
National Geographic," Patti said. "Except for the flies and the
sloppy way lots of things are done there, I enjoyed every minute
of Calcutta. Maybe I just don't see things, but I actually enjoyed
just walking down the streets. It's not that I didn't feel for the
people in the gutter, but you realize that whatever you give them
in a material way won't help much.

"I know they feel as we do. Barefooted or not, the stones hurt
their feet. Even when you get away from them in a hotel room or
something, you can't forget them, but in spite of all that, I enjoyed myself."

Sandy Ragins had once tried to explain the same idea to me.

"Sensitivity is a big thing with all of us," he had said. "Yet
a certain insensitivity is essential. You'd crack up if you finally
didn't get insensitive to beggars and the other things that Indians
themselves pay no attention to. We try not to make comparisons
between India and America, and that helps. We try to consider
India as it is and then, later, relate it to America. I don't feel our
attitudes have been wrong."

Mary Ann Buford, too, was concerned about her own reactions
to Indian misery. She joined Patti and Ruth on the patio and said:

"I've become immune to things here that I would never ignore in the States. At home I never pass a beggar without giving him something. If I did, my conscience would bother me. But here I brush them off.

"I think sometimes we have all been a little too immune. We've had difficulty being ourselves."

"I haven't noticed that very much," I said.

"Oh, I think we've helped here," Mary Ann replied. "One boy said to me that he'd always thought of America as a land of business machines, but now that he'd met us, he had to admit he was amazed—we had so many material things, he said, and still we were friendly and human. I think after a while the students we met will remember us as people who are striving for things in the future just like people anywhere else. We just happened to be born in America."

With a final snip of Ruth Taketaya's scissors, the haircutting session ended. Patti was ready to go. Lerner and I hired bicycle rickshaws, and we rode two miles to the center of Puri. There we found a broad square crowded with merchants, religious pilgrims from all over India, and two gigantic wagons, which were being constructed for Puri's most religious holiday, the June 15th celebration in honor of Jagannath Deb, a Hindu god. A priest told us that the wagons take a whole year to build and are burnt to ashes on that one day.

"Your English word juggernaut comes from this celebration," he said.

Even in skeleton form, the wagons were imposing. On one a lattice-work rose nearly fifty feet in the air, and workmen struggled to build it even higher. On the other a man was painting an intricate red and blue pattern on a spoked wheel. He had just begun and had a long way to go: each wagon had thirty wheels.

Across the square, a high stone wall, perhaps a quarter of a mile long, hid the temple of Jagannath Deb from the eyes of unbelievers. We asked a long-haired priest at the gate to let us in, but his best suggestion was that we find a way to a roof-top on the other side of the street. From there we would be able to see over the wall. He pointed to a likely building, the Puri library. We found the librarian a most agreeable man and were soon on the library roof with him. From where we stood, we could see that the stone wall surrounded a magnificent, pink-domed temple almost as big as the capitol building in Washington, D.C. Although this was the off season, many pilgrims were milling around inside the walls, and we dearly wanted to be in there ourselves. I suggested that we try the back door.

Leaving our rickshaw drivers in the square, Patti, Lerner, and I walked to the end of the front wall, then along the side wall, which was longer and taller. We had entered a bazaar street, and amused shopkeepers hailed us as we went by. At the rear of the temple, we found a second entrance, guarded by two stone lions, with orange bodies and white faces. A dice game was going on under a shade tree by the gate, but when we approached a tall man in a white gown got off his knees and greeted us.

"May we go in?" I asked.

"Are you a Hindu?" he asked, negatively. This was his final answer. It did not occur to me to offer him money, and I doubt that he would have taken it if I had.

"May we take some pictures of your lions?" I asked.

He shook his head to say he did not care. Lerner stationed Patti beside one of the lions. The sun was bright where she stood, but she looked into the glare and smiled. As always happened when Lerner worked with his Leicas, a crowd gathered behind us. The difference in Puri was their hilarity. A man would make a remark and fifty people would laugh; then another remark and more laughter until they were howling just at the thought of what someone would say *next*. They were a wild bunch.

After a while, our tall man in the white gown—he also had a wide streak of red paint on his forehead which seemed to give him status with the crowd—suggested that we take *his* picture. He looked over our heads and into the faces behind us when he spoke. We could feel the crowd agreeing with him that his picture should be taken, and so Lerner agreed, too. This encouraged another man from the dice game to come forward. He was a short fellow with a big bare chest and wooly hair. He stuck both his thumbs up close to my eyes and said, "You wrestle!"

I did not understand.

"You wrestle!" he said again. Then he slapped me on the chest and slapped himself on the chest. With his hands, he indicated that while he and I were wrestling, Lerner should take our picture.

Patti was amused, but Lerner was not; he only wanted to be left alone so he might make more pictures of Patti Price.

The wrestler was insistent. Already he had dropped his *dhoti* and was twirling around in front of the gate, wearing a scanty pair of tights and flexing his muscles. The crowd howled. Someone pushed me in the back. Underneath the uproar, there was another more ominous sound, a sort of angry muttering that no one had to translate for me.

I said hopefully: "Why don't you wrestle with someone else, and we'll take pictures of both of you?" While talking, I made elaborate gestures, which the short man understood.

With one powerful thrust of his right arm, he reached into the crowd, collared a friend, and dragged him into the center of what was now an arena with an audience of about a hundred. The new man stripped down to his underwear, too. Then, with a look toward us to see that the camera was aimed in the proper direction, the men began to wrestle. They waltzed around the circle grappling for position; the short man was the aggressor and his wily friend an expert back-peddler. Suddenly they made contact. The short man grabbed his friend's neck, twisted him down and around and up until their legs and arms were hopelessly entwined and they seemed in imminent danger of crashing to the ground. But they did not fall; they held that exact position and lifted their eyes toward us. They smiled widely for the camera and neither moved nor released their holds until they heard the click of Lerner's shutter.

After four such poses, they had had enough. The crowd cheered them as they replaced their clothing. We decided that this was the time to leave Jagannath Deb temple. Lerner picked up his camera bag and I took Patti's arm, turning her toward the crowd. Standing immovable before us where the two wrestlers and the tall man with the red streak on his forehead, each with a palm up.

"No baksheesh," I said.

The short man screamed, pulled back his hand, screamed louder, and shoved his hand forward again.

"No, no, no." I said.

The short man appealed to the crowd, which agreed that he should be paid—from the noise they made, it seemed as though *all* of them wanted to be paid.

"Just keep walking," I said to Patti and we began to move— around the outstretched hands, through the crowd, and into the clear area beyond. They let us pass and then followed us as we walked, shouting insults, laughing, and making a terrifying fuss.

At the corner, we turned into the bazaar street. The mob stopped there, and we were free.

THE change—from weeks of peace to a moment of violence— was not without humor, but it had its moment of fear, too. We did not mention the incident back at the Eastern Railway Hotel. That night was Gram's birthday party, which all of us had helped plan, so we did not want to spoil it with that story.

The party itself was great fun. We had an elaborate dinner, all of us seated around a single long table. Jaffie had ordered a birthday cake, and each team had pooled its resources to buy gifts. The southern team gave Gram an ivory letter-opener from Trivandrum, while the Calcutta team had splurged on an odd-looking silver and copper jug, which had been made in Tibet. Gram couldn't have been more pleased.

In the morning, Lerner and I rode the train back to Calcutta. Gram and the southern team were on the train with us in another compartment. They were heading for a ten-day session with the college students in Lucknow, a large city northwest of Calcutta in the state of Uttar Pradesh. At the same time, Jaffie and the Calcutta team were on another train going south a few miles to Cuttack, which, like Puri, was in Orissa state. After Cuttack, they were scheduled to go to Patna in Bihar state, again north and west of Calcutta. The teams would meet in New Delhi to begin their return trip.

Our farewells were brief because Lerner and I planned to meet all of them again in Geneva, Switzerland, three weeks hence, where they would stop for a brief rest at the end of the first leg of their journey home.

20 IN CALCUTTA, BOB LERNER AND I HAD A FEW DAYS TO WAIT FOR PLANE CONNECTIONS TO BOMBAY. WE CHECKED IN AT THE GREAT EASTERN HOTEL WHERE GLADLY WE PAID a little extra for the pleasures of an air-conditioned room. It was August 14th, the day before India's Independence Day.

At breakfast on August 16th, I unfolded my copy of *The Statesman,* Calcutta's English language morning paper, which carried the following banner story:

PORTUGUESE KILL 20 SATYAGRAHIS
Belgaum, Aug. 15—Portuguese soldiers fired at *satyagrahis* soon after they crossed the Goa and Daman borders at several points today. According to information reaching the National Congress here late tonight, 20 *satyagrahis* were killed. At least 44 other *satyagrahis* sustained bullet wounds, while many were injured when they were beaten by batons, lathis, and truncheons. . . .

It was a sorry event. Reading about it miles across India in Calcutta, one could hardly believe the Portuguese would fire on the disheveled, unarmed band of *satyagrahis*—non-violent demonstrators—whose pre-Independence Day mobilization meeting was pictured on the front page. For the Portuguese, however, it was an intolerable situation. Goa, they claimed, was rightfully theirs and—armed or not—an invasion is an invasion; so they started shooting. Some Portuguese soldiers even had the bad form to do their killing seated in camp chairs. All Indians, naturally, were incensed, although some thought the Indian Government had not tried hard enough to discourage the *satyagraha*.

Another column in *The Statesman* announced that a *hartal*—a general strike—had been called to protest the shootings. It was set for 8:00 A.M. to 4:00 P.M. on August 17th—the day Lerner and I were due to leave Calcutta. Nothing in the city would move for eight hours, except ambulances and police lorries.

Can a city of six million stand still for a day? It seemed impossible to me.

I remembered, then, the college boy from the Progressive Students Association who had tried to sell me a raffle ticket to benefit the *satyagrahis*. He had assured me that no one was going to be hurt in Goa. I wondered if he had been there on Independence Day and, if he was, did he survive the march? There was no way to find out.

Still another news story in the paper interested me:

RECURRENCE OF STUDENT DISORDERS

Patna, Aug. 15—Two persons were killed and five were wounded when the police fired this morning on a crowd of students in front of the State Transport Depot. According to Patna police, the students set fire to the depot canteen, had indulged in heavy brick-batting, and assaulted the depot officer. The firing was resorted to after lathi charges had failed to disperse the violent crowd . . .

Bob Jaffie and his Project India team were scheduled to go to Patna, so Lerner and I ran over to U.S.I.S. to sound the alarm. Aileen Aderton, the cultural affairs officer, already had wired Jaffie to cancel the Patna trip. He would substitute another town where the college students were not so upset. Miss Aderton also told us that U.S.I.S. would close on August 17th in observance of the *hartal*. American policy was not then involved one way or the other in the Goa affair, but remaining open on *hartal* day would have been construed as American support for the Portuguese— an invitation to destruction of U.S.I.S. property at the hands of the mobs which were expected to patrol Chowringhee Road on the morrow.

On the day of the *hartal*, the dining room deep inside our hotel was opened for business, but the rest of Calcutta was not. At about 10:00 A.M., when the *hartal* was two hours old, Lerner and I walked up to the Maidan. The streets were empty—not a bus, tram, taxi, rickshaw, or ox cart was in sight. In front of the Governor's mansion, the police guard had been doubled. A few scattered loiterers lay on the Maidan grass, but the goatherd had not brought his animals for grazing this morning. The poor and the humble, who carried on all of life's functions on the street corners of Calcutta, had disappeared. They had gone in search

of safety or had joined one of the mobs blockading every intersection of importance that led into the center of the city. For a
day at least, their lives would not be boring or pointless.

Every shop was buttoned up tight. It was like Yom Kippur Day
on the Lower East Side, except that the bank guards and store
police were everywhere on duty in force. Wisely, they had put
away their rifles. If the Portuguese had been equally wise, the
hartal would not have been necessary. They carried more modest
weapons—batons, lathis, and truncheons. A lathi, by the way, is
a steel-tipped hardwood rod, about five feet long, which is swung
like a whip or a baseball bat and is singularly effective in quelling
an unruly crowd.

One bank guard, a man with tiny eyes and a long beard, had
an extra weapon stuck in his belt—a Kashmiri knife two feet long
with a curved blade and an ivory handle. It was unsheathed.

The police patrolled the streets in teams of twelve, riding on
open trucks. They hung on to a single iron bar that ran the length
of the truck bed, bracing themselves with their lathis. They could
jump into a fray instantaneously.

Every hundred feet or so, Lerner and I passed a small group of
men. The men were talking in low voices, waiting for something
to happen. One fellow looked very unhappy to see us and stared
hard at our open collars. It seems that the necktie is a sometime-
symbol of Western colonialism which quickly goes out of fashion
during a *hartal*. A man wearing one is likely to be asked to remove
it or have it ripped off.

An unnatural silence hung over Chowringhee Road. A raven
flew low looking for food and was disappointed. A dog sniffed in
the gutter. A private car was stopped in the middle of the street
and the driver forced to get out and walk. The sun burned away
the clouds—it was Calcutta's luck that it would not rain this day
for the first time in a month. A little rain, the police say, helps
keep order.

Suddenly Lerner and I heard shouting in a side street. We ran
to the corner and watched two or three thousand angry men
stone the Portuguese consulate. A man in white was up on the

roof tearing down the Portuguese flag while, below him, the rabble cheered. They stamped their feet and shook their fists and coughed as the dust rose from the street. The police were not around, being disinclined to fight a battle for the Portuguese.

When we had seen enough of the mob, Lerner and I walked back to our hotel and stayed inside until it was time to go to Dum Dum Airport. Our luggage was loaded onto a bus which had been parked in the alley next to the hotel all day. The driver tuned up his engine and precisely at 4:00 P.M., with twenty Indian passengers, we pulled away from the door and into the empty street. Technically speaking, the *hartal* was over. The question was, did the mob care much for technicalities?

A mile from the hotel, the bus was stopped by about five thousand sullen men and boys. From a tree nearby they had strung up an effigy of Salazar, dictator of Portugal, and were preparing to burn it. For a moment no one moved. We simply were afloat in a sea of humanity which refused to part and let us pass through the intersection. Men began pounding on the side of the bus and shook their fingers at us through the windows. All of them stayed on one side and it did not take long to understand why: if force became necessary, they would have to tip us over, and they would not want to crush any of their own mob.

Our driver began to talk fast. He reasoned, cajoled, threatened, pointed at his watch, read off the passenger list, argued, and held out his hands in prayer. The spokesman for the mob listened calmly. At last he nodded his head; we could go on. The waters parted and we were able to drive two miles more before reaching the next human road block. Our bus driver, having mastered the lingo, was able to talk us through again. In this fitful way, we finally reached Dum Dum.

Air India's plane was waiting for us, and without incident we flew to Bombay, which had been torn up by a *hartal* of its own twenty-four hours earlier. In Bombay, the police were forced to curb some of the more enthusiastic mobs, and it is a question whether more people were killed during the *hartals* than were killed in Goa.

THREE weeks later, in Geneva, Switzerland, Lerner and I were at the airport when Project India landed. Gram, Jaffie, and the twelve students were loaded down with luggage, which was now priceless because it included their souvenirs—paintings by Jamini Roy, the Calcutta artist; brass from New Delhi and ivory from Trivandrum; Madras cloth; figurines from Puri; and all manner of last-minute trinkets from the emporiums of Bombay. Still more things had been sent home by sea to avoid the toll on excess baggage. They were bone tired.

By the time we reached the Hotel Russie, I had heard the details of their most recent exploits. In Lucknow with Gram, Ed Peck's team had had to make its own schedule, a new experience for them considering all the work done by Harold Otwell on their behalf in south India. They were busy for ten straight days, appearing before four thousand students and conducting a seminar, after the pattern set by the Calcutta team. Both Gram and Jerry Lewis had spent five days in bed with fevers, but were feeling better by the time they reached New Delhi.

In Cuttack with Bob Jaffie, Sandy Ragins' team visited seven colleges in three days. They spoke to three thousand students; on their last night in town, fifty stalwarts braved a driving rainstorm to attend a Project India party.

The visit to Patna had been cancelled because of the student riots. In its place, Jaffie arranged for a visit to Allahabad, Pandit Nehru's hometown on the Ganges, not far from Benares. Here the team met with five thousand students during some of the hottest weather—110 degrees—of the summer.

In New Delhi the teams met once more. They were invited to tea by the American ambassador, John Sherman Cooper, and his wife. When they sang the "Star Spangled Banner," Gram reported, she and Mrs. Cooper had a good cry.

Now they were halfway back to California. In the lobby of the hotel, Gram, who hated flying, looked ten years older, but you could tell that she was proud. Her responsibility had been twofold —to the students' families at home and to Project India itself. The latter was fulfilled. During the summer, the twelve students were watched, listened to, and questioned by more than 50,000 young Indians. To the best of their ability, all twelve tried to understand India as well as be understood by it; they forgave and were forgiven many faults. They found the Indian students friendlier than any group of people they had ever met and, in turn, offered them what Asians want most from Westerners—friendship. As for Gram's other responsibility, the odds were good now that she would return all twelve students in reasonably good shape. All they really needed now was a good night's sleep.